CULTS UNCOVERED

TRUE STORIES OF MIND CONTROL AND MURDER

CULTS UNCOVERED

TRUE STORIES OF MIND CONTROL AND MURDER

Written by

Emily G. Thompson

Penguin Random House

Senior Editor Alastair Dougall
Proofreader Kayla Dugger
Designer David McDonald
Jacket Design Lisa Lanzarini
Senior Picture Researcher Sumedha Chopra
Senior Producer Mary Slater
Senior Pre-Production Producer Jennifer Murray
Managing Editor Sarah Harland
Managing Editor Vicky Short
Art Director Lisa Lanzarini
Publisher Julie Ferris

With thanks to Oliver Myers and Victoria Armstrong
for editorial assistance; Nimesh Agrawal for additional picture research.

First American Edition, 2020
Published in the United States by DK Publishing
1450 Broadway, Suite 801, New York, NY 10018

A catalog record for this book is available
from the Library of Congress.

ISBN 978-1-4654-8954-8

DK books are available at special discounts when purchased in bulk for sales
promotions, premiums, fund-raising, or educational use. For details, contact:
DK Publishing Special Markets, 1450 Broadway, Suite 801, New York, NY 10018
SpecialSales@dk.com

Set in 10.5/15pt Bembo MT Pro
Typeset by Jouve (UK), Milton Keynes
Printed and bound in Great Britain by Clays Ltd, Elcograf S.p.A.

A WORLD OF IDEAS:
SEE ALL THERE IS TO KNOW
www.dk.com

Contents

The Oneida Community

Inspired by their messianic leader, these Christian perfectionists dedicated themselves to creating "heaven on Earth." They aspired to live without sin, but their attitudes toward sex breached two of civilized society's most fundamental taboos: incest and sex with children.

———————————

"They wanted to bring heaven to Earth, but Plan A was taking too long, so they started on a Plan B…"

Anthony Wonderly, Curator of the

Oneida Community Mansion

———————————

More than a century has passed since the Oneida Community disbanded. Nevertheless, whispers still linger in the state of New York concerning the abnormal sexual behaviors practiced by this utopian cult. Its leader, John Humphrey Noyes, was born into a prominent local family in Brattleboro, Vermont, on September 3, 1811. His father, John Noyes, was once Vermont's representative to Congress, and his mother, Polly Hayes, was the aunt of President Rutherford B. Hayes.[1] In 1830, Noyes graduated from Dartmouth College, New Hampshire. Abandoning plans to study law after attending an evangelical revival meeting in Putney, Vermont, he went to study at the Andover Theological Seminary, Massachusetts. At Andover, Noyes was dismayed by his colleagues' "lack of spiritual seriousness," so he packed his bags and moved to Yale Theological Seminary, Connecticut.[2] While a student at Yale, Noyes had a vision that convinced him that it was possible to live a life without sin and thus attain perfection. Noyes himself recorded in *Religious Experience of John Humphrey Noyes*, compiled and edited by his son, George Wallingford Noyes, and published in 1923: "I listlessly opened my Bible and my eye fell upon these words: 'The Holy Ghost shall come upon thee, and the power of the highest shall overshadow thee, therefore also that holy thing which shall be born of thee shall be called the Son of God.' These words seemed to glow upon the page, and my spirit heard a voice from Heaven through them promising the baptism of the Holy Spirit and the second birth."

Henceforth, Noyes devoted himself to the unorthodox Christian doctrine of perfectionism—a movement that believed that only those who were free of sin were true Christians. At the time, Yale had a reputation as a haven for progressive-minded Christians; nevertheless, in 1834, Noyes—who declared himself free of sin, and thus in a state of perfection—was kicked out and branded a heretic. For the next few years, Noyes was a spiritual nomad, publishing a number of Christian perfectionist pamphlets. These garnered sufficient interest for Noyes to gather a number of followers. Noyes; his wife Harriet Holton, whom he married in 1838; and his adherents followed the New Testament model of the early church. They all lived together at the Noyes' homestead in Putney. However, their neighbors didn't approve of the group's highly unconventional social arrangements. In 1847, with a charge of adultery hanging over him, Noyes led his acolytes away from Vermont and settled on the shores of Oneida Creek, New York. There, on February 1, 1848, he established the Oneida Community.

Noyes and the Oneida Community believed that Christian theologians had misinterpreted the Bible and that the Second Coming of Christ had already occurred, taking place at the time of the destruction of the Temple of Jerusalem in 70 CE. They believed that a perfect life was possible and that it was their duty to build a new Eden on Earth and strive to eliminate selfishness and sin.

Noyes later claimed, in an 1872 pamphlet, that the Putney group's main work between 1834 and 1846 had been to "develop the religion of the New Covenant and establish union with God." On their rural spot of land about 100 miles (160 km) west of Albany, New York, the Oneida Community set about realizing the second phase of Noyes' brand of Christian perfectionism: "Laying the foundation of a new state of society by developing the true theory of sexual morality." They built a wooden complex they named the Mansion House and mainly supported themselves through agriculture, selling canned fruit, vegetables, cereals, and meat. The Community practiced "Bible Communism," which meant sharing everything—worldly possessions, children, and sexual partners. Members abstained from alcohol, tobacco, and caffeine. They held no regular worship, but instead organized Bible study groups and private meditation sessions. Knowledge and recreational life at Oneida was highly valued. The community had a library and school where members studied a number of languages, as well as classical science and literature. At night, they held educational lectures on a variety of topics, including German philosophy and music. Thirteen boys born in the Oneida Community would go to Yale University.[3] Members spent their free time playing baseball or croquet and conducted theatrical productions, inviting the locals to performances. When asked what the purpose of the Oneida Community was, Noyes simply responded: "The object is to make a happy home."[4]

The Oneida Community challenged social views on property ownership, gender roles, and monogamous marriage. Community members practiced "complex marriage," which meant that they shared sexual partners, in accordance with Noyes' dictum: "Each is married to all." Monogamy and celibacy were not permitted, and so-called "special love" for a specific person was forbidden. Noyes said that monogamy would lead to jealousy, possessiveness, and sin and would put a couple's interests above those of the community. "The two home-spoilers are death and marriage," he

5

claimed.[3] While sex was declared a "community affair," liaisons between members had to be approved by a committee. To prevent unwanted pregnancies, the men of the community practiced continence—meaning that they were forbidden to climax—as a form of birth control. "It is as foolish and cruel to expend one's seed on a wife merely for the sake of getting rid of it, as it would be to fire a gun at one's best friend merely for the sake of unloading it," wrote Noyes in his pamphlet on the subject of male continence. Masturbation was also prohibited because Noyes said it drained spiritual energy. Children were raised communally to prevent their true mothers and fathers from developing "idolatrous" love for them. Noyes emphasized that children at Oneida belonged to God and the community, not their parents.

The Oneida Community began as a handful of followers but quickly transformed into a self-contained group of around 300. During the height of the community's existence, thousands of tourists visited the Mansion House, paying 60 cents for a vegetarian dinner or 25 cents for an evening of "grand entertainment," including music and a puppet show.[5] The Oneida Community were always very open about their practices. Members recorded their daily life in journals, which they published and sent to whomever wanted to read them. (In 1947, the majority of these journals were burned.)

While the Oneida Community had its positive aspects, its perfectionist philosophy intrinsically contained negative ones. Those who took what was perceived as too much of an interest in anything—such as music or literature—were accused of being egotistical or having "prima donna fever."[6] One member, Frank Wayland-Smith, was ordered to give up his violin because, although music reigned supreme among the arts, Noyes felt Wayland-Smith

6

loved music more than the community. Children were ordered to ceremonially burn their favorite dolls in a bid to overcome the "doll spirit," which Noyes said was a form of "graven image" worship.

Of far more serious significance, however, were some of the community's sexual practices. The rule of "ascending fellowship" called for young members to be sexually paired with their elders. According to Noyes, this had many spiritual benefits. Noyes himself took on the task of initiating virgins, some as young as 13, into the community's system of "complex marriage." It was often the duty of the elder women in the community to teach teenage boys the technique of male continence. This way, if they failed, they did not risk an unwanted pregnancy.

Another of the community's most controversial aspects was its eugenics program, during which 58 children were born. Having studied Charles Darwin's theories of natural selection, Noyes created the "stirpiculture" program. This involved the selective breeding of men and women to procreate a second generation of children who would have superior qualities. "They wanted to bring heaven to Earth, but Plan A was taking too long, so they started on a Plan B, which was a eugenics program," commented Anthony Wonderly, curator of the Oneida Community Mansion House, in 2011.[7] Noyes fathered 10 children, while another 19 were his blood relatives. A number of births were the result of uncle-niece unions and, according to Ellen Wayland-Smith in her book *Oneida: From Free Love Utopia to the Well-Set Table,* Noyes contemplated father-daughter and brother-sister relations.

The Oneida Community also practiced "mutual criticism." Community members would gather in small groups to have their personal weaknesses evaluated. "Oneidans were criticized for insincerity, egotism, obstinacy, self-righteousness, frivolity, pride, excessive concern with bodily health, and failing to open their hearts up to God. Critics also paid close attention to defects in manners and social bearing," wrote Spencer Klaw in his book *Without Sin: The Life and Death of the Oneida Community.*[8]

As the Industrial Revolution swept the US during the mid-19th century, it forced a number of changes in self-sufficient communities. In its wake, the Oneida Community changed focus from agriculture to manufacturing and marketing. It launched a successful production line of steel traps, clamps, and chains. "Noyes didn't really like the idea of animal traps, but he didn't like the idea of the community starving to death, either," explained Lang Hatcher, Noyes' great-grandson.[9] The trap shop became the backbone of the community, and Oneida's animal traps came to dominate the market; professional trappers would accept no other brand. In 1866, Oneida also began making silk thread and, later, tin-plated spoons and outdoor furniture.

In many ways, the Oneida Community functioned well as a utopian society and, by the standards of the time, the status of women was extremely progressive. Within the community, women and men were treated equally, taking on the same roles and reaping the same benefits. Moreover, women were free from the shackles of constant pregnancy owing to the practice of male continence. "Men and women will mingle like boys and girls in their employment and labor will become sport," declared Noyes.[1] Moreover, women were free to refuse a man's attention, and the man had to accept the rejection. Working conditions were said to be excellent, and community-produced products were much in demand. By 1870, the Oneida Community was one of the largest employers in the area, with over 200 people on its payroll.[8]

The decline of the Oneida Community began in the early 1880s when a local minister, Dr. John W. Mears, started preaching that the community was immoral. He invited churches from across the state to a secret convention "to right a great wrong."[10] The convention was well attended, and Mears subsequently created a petition to have the Oneida Community abolished by a special act of the legislature. The negative backlash worked and, in 1881, the Oneida Community disbanded. After the dissolution, many community members abandoned the community and moved elsewhere. Some members stayed at the Mansion House and some worked for Oneida Ltd. In June 1879, Noyes fled to Canada, fearing that he would be arrested on adultery and fornication charges. By this point, the religious zeal that had sustained the community had dissipated, and no leader had emerged to replace Noyes. He lived in exile in a stone cottage at Niagara Falls, Ontario, until his death, on April 13, 1886.

The Oneida Community is widely regarded as one of the most successful utopian communities in American history, outlasting similar groups that sprang up in the US during the same period. Following the community's disbandment, its assets were formed into a joint-stock company called Oneida Ltd., which became one of the world's largest silverware and tableware companies.

Oneida Ltd. remains a flourishing family business. The Mansion House is now run by the nonprofit educational group Oneida Community Mansion House, Inc. The 300-room mansion consists of 35 apartments, 10 hotel rooms, and 10 dormitory rooms, as well as a museum. Richard Kathmann, director of the Oneida Mansion House, summed up the heyday of the Oneida Community this way: "Oneida is a powerful example of how people struggle with the idea of God and their relationship to God, and how to deal with two primal passions: sex and the desire for property and power."

---

[1] *Rutland Herald*, 19 October 2002—"History: John Humphrey Noyes and his Utopian Settlement"

[2] *Oneida: From Free Love Utopia to the Well-Set Table* by Ellen Wayland-Smith

[3] *News & Record*, January 9, 1994—"Attempting to Establish a Haven on Earth"

[4] *Cedar Vale Commercial*, August 31, 1889—"Oneida Community"

[5] *The Buffalo News*, January 6, 2008—"Mansion House Recalls the Days of Utopian Community"

[6] *Watertown Daily Times*, September 25, 1994—"Utopia With a Foundation of "Free Love"

[7] *Observer-Dispatch*, October 27, 2011—"Oneida Mansion Houses Controversy"

[8] *Without Sin: The Life and Death of the Oneida Community* by Spencer Klaw

[9] *The Post-Standard*, September 19, 2004—"With Oneida Ltd."

[10] *The Good Silver* by Matthew Dunn

The Manson Family

In January 1971, Charles Manson became the leering face of evil on front pages all over the world. The savage, senseless murders he masterminded shattered the peace and love idealism of the previous decade's "flower power" era.

"You don't have to answer to anybody,

you can be whatever you want to be."

Charles Manson

More than five decades have passed since young followers of shaggy-haired, failed-rock-star-turned-psychopath Charles Manson murdered actress Sharon Tate and six other strangers in two upscale neighborhoods in Hollywood, California. Although he did not commit the actual crimes himself, Manson remains one of the most infamous figures in American criminal history. His complex, predatory personality and the activities of his notorious "Family" have inspired a plethora of books, movies, songs, and documentaries.

Charles Milles Manson was born on November 12, 1934, in Cincinnati, Ohio. His 16-year-old single mother, Kathleen Maddox, did not name her baby for several weeks, during which time he was known as "no-name Maddox." His biological father was a known con artist named Colonel Walker Henderson Scott Sr., who never met his son. The name "Manson" came from his mother's brief marriage to a man named William Manson.

By his own account, Charles Manson's childhood was bleak. He asserted that his mother Kathleen was a sex worker and heavy drinker who made it clear that her little son was unwanted. On one occasion she supposedly tried to sell him to a barmaid for a pitcher of beer.[1] It should be noted that there are no records of her ever being charged or arrested for soliciting. Vincent Bugliosi in his book *Helter Skelter: The True Story of the Manson Murders* quotes a relative saying that Kathleen was not a sex worker but "loose."

When Charles was five years old, Kathleen was jailed for taking part in a botched armed robbery with her brother. Charles was sent to live with a religious aunt and uncle and his cousin, JoAnn. She recalled that the innocent-looking boy had a darker side, describing him as an attention-seeking habitual liar prone to tantrums. While in high school, Manson used to recruit gullible classmates—mostly girls—to attack students he didn't like.[2]

In 1942, Kathleen was released on parole and went to fetch her son. Manson later recollected that that day was the sole happy moment of his entire childhood. However, this spell of family bliss didn't last. Kathleen decided she couldn't handle her young son and shipped him off to the Gibault School, a "home for wayward boys" in Terre Haute, Indiana. Charles escaped and tracked down his mother, who turned him away at the door. He spent much of the rest of his childhood in and out of penal institutions, where he was assaulted, both physically and sexually, by the other boys, most of whom towered over his small frame. (As an adult, Manson was only 5 ft 2 in (1.6 m) tall.)

Years of petty crime followed. Manson was variously convicted of stealing cars, robbing petrol stations, and parole and probation violations. He also married twice. His first wife was waitress Rosalie Jean Willis (wed 1955; divorced 1958), by whom he fathered a son, Charles Manson Jr. His second wife was sex worker Leona Rae Musser (married 1959; divorced 1963). During his various spells in jail, Manson took little interest in acquiring a useful trade on one of the various rehabilitative programmes on offer. However, a course based on Dale Carnegie's best-selling 1936 book *How to Win Friends and Influence People* fully captured his attention. Manson fully absorbed Carnegie dictums, such as: "The only way to influence the other fellow is to talk about what he wants and show him how to get it"; "use showmanship . . . if you want attention"; and "make the other person feel important." While doing time for forging a $37.50 check and parole violation at McNeil Island, Washington, in the early 1960s, Manson had rudimentary guitar lessons courtesy of a fellow convict named Alvin "Creepy" Karpis. Manson began writing songs of his own and dreamed of making it big like his heroes The Beatles, whose fame was sweeping the nation. A friendship with music business insider Phil Kaufman, in jail for drug possession, fueled Manson's rock star fantasies.

On March 21, 1967, Manson—who had spent half of his 32 years in correctional facilities—was released from prison after serving a six-year sentence for forging a $37 check and violating parole. Manson had begged not to be released. "I know I won't be able to adjust in the world, not after I spent all my life locked up and my mind was free," he said.[3]

Manson headed for San Francisco's Haight-Ashbury district, a nexus of countercultural lifestyles attracting teenage runaways, idealists, charlatans, and drug dealers. With his piercing eyes; jailhouse smarts; controlling, compelling personality; and modicum of talent as a guitar player and singer, he found it easy to dazzle impressionable teenagers, especially girls, with his fantasies of becoming a rock star in the Los Angeles music scene.

Once in the "City of Angels," however, Manson had trouble standing out from the crowd of hippies who had washed up in LA seeking fame and fortune in the record business. A break came when he was introduced to Dennis Wilson of the Beach Boys by Gary Hinman, a UCLA chemistry graduate, scenester, music teacher, and multi-instrumentalist. Manson impressed the well-connected, wealthy, but somewhat naive Wilson. "Dennis really took Charlie under his wing," said former Manson acolyte Dianne Lake, author of *Member of the Family: My Story of Charles Manson*. "Charlie was teaching Dennis how to play the guitar and I think he admired Charlie."[4] Manson allegedly provided Dennis Wilson and other musicians with drugs and women to take part in orgies. These claims were backed up by Beach Boys recording engineer Steven Desper. "Dennis and Charlie and all these girls were in this whole thing together," he said.

Manson and Wilson's friendship turned sour after Wilson scheduled a recording session for Manson in the summer of 1968, which fellow Beach Boy Mike Love also attended. When Manson didn't get his way, he pulled out a knife and threatened Wilson and Love. Manson was subsequently rejected by numerous insiders, including record producer Terry Melcher, film star Doris Day's son, who attempted to record some of Manson's half-completed songs before abandoning the idea. Melcher had also floated the idea of making a documentary that would highlight Manson's music, but changed his mind after witnessing Manson getting involved in a fight with a drunk. Melcher's rejection did not go down well with Manson.

One of Manson's songs, "Cease to Exist," was recorded by the Beach Boys for their 1968 album *20/20*. However, it was revised by Dennis Wilson, retitled "Never Learn Not to Love," and Manson was uncredited, further fueling his feelings of resentment, paranoia, and alienation.

While Manson faced rejection by LA's musical "aristocracy"—who ultimately found his outsider shtick, though superficially interesting, just too weird to be commercial—the political and social upheavals of 1960s California had created the ideal conditions for a "hippie guru" to flourish. Manson had gained a number of devoted followers who were disenchanted with their lives. They were young, impressionable "rebels without a cause," running from a world wracked by bitter clashes over US involvement in the Vietnam War, civil rights tensions, and intergenerational battles. Manson and his acolytes used to drive an old school bus between San Francisco and Los Angeles to pick up runaway youngsters, forming what would become his Family. Many were girls attracted by his weird charisma. "We were just a bunch of kids looking for love and attention and a different way to live," recalled Family member Catherine Share.[5] Family member Leslie Van Houten, who started taking LSD at the age of 16, recalled in 1977 that Manson was "very dominant . . . More than anything else, he was the only one who knew what he was doing . . . he was a free person, free of inhibition . . . a pied piper . . . a really good con artist." Plying his Family with LSD, marijuana, and other drugs; encouraging orgies and free love; engaging in sing-alongs; and exerting control over every aspect of their lives, Manson had a remarkable ability to influence young minds—a "gift" that would later see him referred to as "the devil" by the more sensationalist media outlets.

Initially, Manson and his slavish female followers stayed at various locations, including a house in Canoga Park, California, called the "yellow submarine," remote Barker Ranch in Death Valley, and Dennis Wilson's luxurious home in Rustic Canyon. After being evicted from Wilson's home by his manager, the Family continued their life of sex, drugs, and rock'n'roll in Spahn Ranch, a former western movie set just outside Los Angeles. At

Spahn Ranch, Charles Manson found his own kind of stardom. Family member Patricia Krenwinkel later recalled him playing his guitar or flute while his naked "loves" flocked and danced around him "like wood nymphs and wood creatures." Jonathan Shaw, a teenager who met Manson at the ranch in the late 1960s, recollected life at Spahn Ranch: "We sat around with a bunch of kids, smoking pot and singing songs. Manson was there playing a guitar and everyone was singing along," he said. "He looked very cool, like an Indian chief."

In summer, Manson and the Family slept outside in nearby fields and the woods; during the winter, they slept in one of the movie set's abandoned buildings. During the day, they sewed clothing, walked in the mountains, or went on "garbage trips" to collect anything they could make use of. According to Linda Kasabian, who came to Spahn Ranch after her husband abandoned her and her son, "We lived as mother, father, and children. We were all one."

At night, they played musical instruments, sang, danced, and raced motorcycles on Santa Susanna Pass Road. When neighbors complained, they were threatened with violence. The Family was allowed to stay on Spahn Ranch quite simply because people were afraid of them. "I couldn't get rid of them," said George Spahn, the elderly, blind owner of the ranch.

Orgies were a common occurrence. Several young women had babies that other members of the Family delivered themselves. "You're brought up to believe that you can't have sex unless you're married," said one girl who was close to the Family. "Here, girls could do whatever they wanted; they didn't have to worry about getting caught or toeing the mark. Charlie always said 'You don't have to answer to anybody, you can be whatever you want to be.'"

Before long, the Spahn Ranch commune, cut off from anything

even faintly resembling societal norms, became a breeding ground for Manson's pent-up venom. A virulent racist, he became preoccupied by a white supremacist, apocalyptic vision of a coming war between black and white Americans. Manson self-identified as Jesus Christ and became obsessed with what he believed were hidden messages hidden in the lyrics of The Beatles' "White Album," released on November 22, 1968. In particular, Manson interpreted the song "Helter Skelter" as a vision of the coming apocalypse. During communal LSD trips, he convinced the Family that they were going to find a hole in the ground in Death Valley that would be a sanctuary for him and the Family during the imminent war. After black people had defeated white people, Manson and his Family would emerge, armed and riding customized dune buggies to take over and rule. The following year, tired of waiting for his "Helter Skelter" race war to begin, Manson decided to instigate it and put the blame on the Black Panthers, a key political organization campaigning for African American civil rights.

On July 25, 1969, Manson ordered three of his followers—Bobby Beausoleil, Mary Brunner, and Susan Atkins—to go to the Topanga Canyon home of Gary Hinman. A practicing Buddhist said to be a "kind, gentle soul," Hinman had often allowed Family members to crash at his home. There are conflicting stories as to Manson's motives—some say Manson believed that Hinman had come into money and wanted him to turn his assets over to the Family, while others say that Hinman had sold the Family some bad mescaline. Hinman was held hostage at gunpoint by the three Family members for two days before Manson showed up, armed with a sword. Hinman pleaded that he was Manson's friend and that he had no money to give him—he had already signed over the pink slips to both of his cars to Manson's right-hand man, Charles

"Tex" Watson, before Manson arrived. Unappeased, Manson slashed Hinman across the face with the sword, almost severing his ear. "You know what to do," said Manson, before leaving Hinman's residence.[6] After Manson left, Atkins and allegedly Brunner held a pillow over Hinman's face while Beausoleil stabbed him several times. As Hinman lay dying, Beausoleil dipped his hand in Hinman's blood, wrote "POLITICAL PIGGY" (referencing the George Harrison song "Piggies" from the "White Album"), and drew a paw print on the wall to make it seem as though the Black Panthers had committed the murder. Beausoleil would later claim that it was Atkins who did this. On August 6, he was arrested and charged with the murder after he was found sleeping in Hinman's Fiat, which had broken down on the highway at Cuesta Grade.

Hinman's death was just the first in what would become a series of savage murders committed by the Manson Family. On a warm summer night on August 8, 1969, Tex Watson, Susan Atkins, and Patricia Krenwinkel arrived at 10050 Cielo Drive in Benedict Canyon. A fourth Family member, Linda Kasabian, was getaway driver. 10050 Cielo Drive was the elegant house where Manson had met with record producer Terry Melcher when Melcher was thinking of recording Manson's songs. Melcher had been living there with his film star girlfriend Candice Bergen. They had split up earlier in the year; Melcher was now living in Malibu, and the house was being rented by movie director Roman Polanski and his pregnant film star wife Sharon Tate, best known as tragic starlet Jennifer North in 1967's *Valley of the Dolls*. Polanski was away, working on a film project in England.

Manson's motives for targeting the occupants of 10050 Cielo Drive are open to debate. It has been speculated that he thought that Melcher was still living there and wanted revenge for being turned down. Tex Watson, in his 1978 book *Will You Die for Me?*, recalled, "More than ever, Terry Melcher, in his house at the top of Cielo Drive, with his power and his money was the focus for the bitterness and sense of betrayal that some of the Family felt for all those phoney Hollywood hippies who kept silencing the truth Charlie had to share. These 'beautiful people,' Terry and all the others, who were really no different from the rich piggies in their white shirts and ties and suits. And just like them, they too deserved a 'damn good whacking.'"

It is probable that Manson knew that Melcher had left town and did not really care who was actually living in the house, provided they were wealthy "beautiful people." Butchering them would guarantee greater public outcry, and therefore help foment his goal of a race war. According to Watson, Manson said, "Now is the time for Helter Skelter," and told Watson, Susan Atkins, and Patricia Krenwinkel to "totally destroy everyone in that house, as gruesome as you can."

As Watson, Atkins, and Krenwinkel, high on speed and cocaine, approached the house, they came across 18-year-old Steven Parent. He had been visiting with the caretaker of the home, William Garretson, who lived in the property's guesthouse. Parent was leaving in his car when he was shot and stabbed four times by Tex Watson. Watson then entered the main house, announcing "I am the devil, and I'm here to do the devil's work."[7] All the occupants— Sharon Tate, celebrity hairdresser and Sharon's close friend Jay Sebring, coffee heiress Abigail Folger, and her partner and Polanski's friend, aspiring screenwriter Wojciech Frykowski—were hauled out of their bedrooms and brought into the living room, where they were tied up with towels. Sebring was forced to lie face down before being shot by Watson. As he struggled for breath, Watson kicked him in the face over and over again. Realizing that the three hippie intruders were there not to rob, but to murder, mass panic ensued. Frykowski got free and started to struggle with Atkins before being stabbed in the legs. He staggered outside and Watson shot him twice and stabbed him repeatedly. Standing on the lawn, Linda Kasabian looked on in horror. She later claimed that she ran back to the car but dared not drive away for fear of what would happen to her young son, who was at the Family's Spahn Ranch.

According to an interview with Susan Atkins in the *Winnipeg Free Press*, December 20, 1969, inside the house, Atkins had Tate—who was eight-and-a-half months pregnant—in a headlock. "She began begging me to let her go so she could have her baby and, wow, I realized she was pregnant. A flash in the midst of all that!" Krenwinkel was struggling to subdue Abigail Folger, and Atkins called out to Tex Watson to "do something." He stabbed Folger, who staggered outside; Watson pursued her and killed her. He then came back inside and told Atkins to kill Tate. Atkins claimed that she was unwilling to kill Tate herself, but she grabbed ahold of Tate's arms and Watson stabbed her several times. Atkins commented: "And when it was all over, I didn't want to go back in that house, but something made me go. I went over to Sharon Tate, and I flashed, wow, there's a living being in there. I wanted to, but I couldn't bring myself to cut her open and take the baby. I knew it was living, I knew it wouldn't." Atkins then recalled dipping a towel in Tate's blood and using it to smear "Pig" on the front door. Police later estimated that the Family had been in the mansion for about 25 minutes.

Manson Family trial prosecutor Victor Bugliosi would later claim in his book *Helter Skelter* that Susan Atkins herself stabbed

Tate 16 times and that the bodies of Tate and Sebring were tied together and hung from ceiling beams in the living room. The latter statement was confirmed by police crime scene photos. He also stated that Atkins tasted Tate's blood and said it was "warm and sticky, and nice."

According to Atkins' 1969 account, after the murders, the trio then went to find Linda Kasabian, who was waiting in the car. While they drove away, they changed out of their bloodstained clothes, which they threw along with their weapons "down a ravine." They then drove around until they found a "dark house." They began using a garden hose to wash the blood off themselves. An old couple came out of the house and asked them what they were doing. "We're just getting a drink of water. Sorry we disturbed you," Watson explained. The couple were still suspicious, but Watson, Atkins, and Krenwinkel managed to get back to their car and drive off. After visiting a gas station to refuel and to check for remaining blood traces in the station's restroom, they returned to the Family's ranch. Fearful that the car still contained traces of blood, Atkins took a rag from the kitchen and set about cleaning it inside and out. "Charlie and Tex told me I would be killed if I betrayed their trust," she recalled "But it made no difference to me. Charlie was me and I was Charlie, and all of us were one at the ranch."

The grisly scene at Cielo Drive was discovered the following morning by housekeeper Winifred Chapman. As news of the murders broke and all of Hollywood reeled in shock, Manson was reportedly unhappy with how sloppy the previous night's killings had been. According to Manson, Watson had messed up by letting the victims know that they were going to be killed and causing panic. To show the Family how to murder more efficiently, Manson accompanied the same four killers plus Family member Leslie Van Houten to 3301 Waverly Drive, where Leno and Rosemary LaBianca lived. Mr. LaBianca was an army veteran who had built up a successful supermarket business, while Mrs. LaBianca co-owned a local dress shop. The couple had just returned from vacation when Manson and his followers showed up at their home. Manson and Watson tied Mr. LaBianca up at gunpoint. Claiming they were only there to rob them, they took Mrs. LaBianca to the bedroom and tied her up as well. The two men ransacked the house before placing a pillowcase over Mr. LaBianca's head and gagging him with a lamp cord. Manson then reportedly left the residence, telling the others to "paint a picture more gruesome than anyone has ever seen."[8] The family did just that. Sensing what was about to come, Mr. LaBianca started to struggle and scream. Watson responded by stabbing him in the throat with a chrome-plated bayonet. He continued to stab Mr. LaBianca, who reportedly gurgled "I'm dead, I'm dead," until Watson was satisfied that he really was. Mrs. LaBianca, who could hear the commotion from the bedroom, had been gagged and hooded with a pillow case. She tried to escape from the bedroom but was stabbed several times by Krenwinkel. Watson then entered the room and stabbed her in the chest and neck until she stopped moving. The killers then carved the word "WAR" into Mr. LaBianca's stomach, jammed a fork in beside it, and thrust a knife into his throat. In the blood of their victims, they then scribbled "DEATH TO PIGS" on the wall and "HEALTER SKELTER" [sic] on the refrigerator. The motive for the murders remains obscure; it is possible that the LaBiancas were targeted simply because the Family had previously attended a party at the house next door.

After the LaBianca murders, Manson drove Linda Kasabian

to a black neighborhood and told her to dispose of Mrs. LaBianca's purse. He hoped that a black person would find it, use Mrs. LaBianca's credit card, and be linked to the murders.

In just two nights, the Family's explosion of violence diverted the world's attention from the bloody war in Vietnam to the senseless slaughter of Hollywood's beautiful and wealthy elite. The killings sent shockwaves across the US, particularly California. People locked their doors and bolted their windows while the killers remained at large. For almost three months, investigators collected evidence but made next to no progress. However, in October, police visited another Family hangout, Barker Ranch, and arrested several members for auto theft. One of them was Susan Atkins, who subsequently confessed that she, Bobby Beausoleil, and Charles Manson were responsible for the murder of Gary Hinman. The following month, Atkins—now under arrest for Hinman's murder—made another confession. In gruesome detail, Atkins claimed she had participated in Sharon Tate's murder, "Because we wanted to do a crime that would shock the world, that the world would have to stand up and take notice."[9]

Spahn Ranch was raided, and officers found Manson hiding in a cupboard under a sink. Tex Watson was arrested in Texas; however, he would not be brought to trial for a further nine months while his lawyers fought extradition to California.

The Manson Family trial—Manson plus Susan Atkins, Patricia Krenwinkel, and Leslie Van Houten—began on June 16, 1970. The case, a cocktail of murder, celebrities, sex, and drugs, held particular allure for the world's media. During the nine-month trial—which prosecuting counsel Vincent Bugliosi referred to as "the most bizarre, savage, and nightmarish in the history of crime"—Manson and his followers staged several bizarre outbursts.

"These children that come at you with knives, they are your children," said Manson in one courtroom soliloquy. At one point, he launched himself across the counsel table at the judge; at others, his female followers giggled, sang, and chanted in unison. One day, Manson and his co-defendants entered the courtroom with an "X" carved into their foreheads. According to Manson, they had been "Xed out of society." On another occasion, Manson entered the courtroom with his head shaved; once again, his co-defendants followed suit. Outside the courthouse, some of Manson's remaining followers camped out and threatened self-immolation if he was convicted. Meanwhile, inside the courtroom, the shocking details of the killings were emerging, largely thanks to former Family member Linda Kasabian, who had been offered immunity from prosecution in exchange for her testimony.

After initially pleading innocent, the women on trial finally confessed that they and Tex Watson had committed the murders. Atkins now claimed that she had stabbed Tate herself: "I just stabbed her and she fell and I stabbed her again. I don't know how many times. I don't know why I stabbed her." She also said she was "stoned on acid" at the time and could remember few details about the murders. [10]

In his book, *Will You Die for Me?*, Tex Watson took full responsibility for Sharon Tate's murder. He recalled that Tate was sitting on the sofa with Susan Atkins and that she begged to be taken to the Family's ranch so she could have her baby before being killed. "It was the first time I realized she was pregnant, and for a moment it almost seemed like a good idea." However, urged on by "Katie" (Patricia Krenwinkel) and his memories of Manson's instructions, and aware that Atkins was "just sat there holding Sharon," Watson murdered Tate. "Later, Prosecutor Bugliosi, because of some things

Susan-Sadie bragged about in jail in one of her attempts to get attention, was convinced that it was she who killed Sharon Tate, but his suspicion was not true. It was my hand that struck out, over and over . . ."

Van Houten—who wasn't present at the Tate house—admitted to stabbing Mrs. LaBianca, but only after she was already dead. In an act of true devotion, the women tried to absolve Manson of any guilt. The evidence against Manson was mostly circumstantial, and Manson maintained his innocence throughout. He also emphatically denied that he had encouraged his followers to commit murder. "I have killed no one and I have ordered no one to be killed," he said.[11] However, prosecution counselor Bugliosi, a little-known deputy district attorney before being handed the case that would define his career, convincingly argued that Manson ordered the killings because he wanted to foment a race war. Inspired by his deluded reading of The Beatles song "Helter Skelter," Manson believed that African Americans would rise as the new majority race in a gruesome battle fueled by racial tension. He also maintained that, in the aftermath, he and his followers would take over as the leaders of the African American race.[12] These details were confirmed at the trial by former Family member Paul Watkins. Others have claimed that Manson ordered the murders as revenge against record producer Terry Melcher, who had lived at 10050 Cielo Drive before subletting it to Tate and Polanski. Susan Atkins would later say, "Charles picked that house to instill fear into Terry Melcher, because Terry had given us his word on a few things and never came through with them."

On March 29, 1971, Manson and the three women were found guilty and sentenced to death. As well as the Tate-LaBianca murders, Manson was found guilty of killing Gary Hinman and stuntman

Donald "Shorty" Shea, who worked at Spahn Ranch. (Manson allegedly believed Shea had reported the Family to police.) Susan Atkins later claimed that Manson had planned to murder Elizabeth Taylor, Richard Burton, Tom Jones, and Steve McQueen. The latter had actually been invited to dinner at 10050 Cielo Drive that night, but cancelled at the last minute.

Watson—who was tried separately—was also found guilty and received a death sentence. The previous year, Bobby Beausoleil had been found guilty of the murder of Gary Hinman and also sentenced to death. However, in 1972, California abolished capital punishment and the sentences were commuted to life imprisonment.

Over the ensuing years, the Manson Family sporadically attended parole hearings, vainly hoping to be granted freedom. Those convicted alongside Manson denounced him and expressed remorse for their willingness to be brainwashed into committing such savage acts.

Leslie Van Houten, reportedly a model prisoner, was recommended for parole in April 2016. However, the decision was reversed by California governor Jerry Brown, and his decision was upheld by a Los Angeles Superior Court judge. In January 2019, she was recommended for parole once again, but in June, this was overruled by governor Gavin Newsom. Explaining his decision, he wrote: "While I commend Ms. Van Houten for her efforts at rehabilitation and acknowledge her youth at the time of the crimes, I am concerned about her role in these killings and her potential for future violence."

Charles "Tex" Watson became a born-again Christian (in 1975) and ordained minister, as well as fathering four children during conjugal visits. He has been denied parole 17 times, the most recent in 2016.

Patricia Krenwinkel has also reportedly been a model prisoner. She earned a bachelor's and master's degree in counseling and runs rehabilitation programs for offenders.

Susan Atkins was married twice and converted to Christianity while serving her sentence. In a 1976 interview, she persisted in her claim that Watson had committed all the murders at Cielo Drive. Atkins was denied parole 13 times and died of brain cancer in 2009.

Manson Family member Lynette "Squeaky" Fromme was arrested in 1975 after attempting to assassinate President Gerald Ford. At the time, she was living in Sacramento because it was close to Folsom Prison, where Manson was being held. She was released from prison in 2009.

In November 2017, Charles Manson died from cardiac arrest resulting from respiratory failure and colon cancer at California State Prison. He was 83. He never confessed to his part in the murders and showed no remorse for them. While in prison, he changed the "X" carved on his forehead into a swastika. "Maybe I should have killed 500 people," he said in an interview in 1987. "Then I would have felt better. Then I would have felt like I really offered society something." While incarcerated, he allegedly received more than 60,000 letters per year.

An album of Manson's songs was released in March 1970. It was named *Lie: The Love and Terror Cult* and included songs such as "Garbage Dump," Sick City," "Look at Your Game, Girl," as well as "Cease to Exist." His songs have since been covered by bands such as Guns N' Roses and The Lemonheads, with royalties going to the victims under a court order.

The Manson Family murders exposed the violent and drug-riddled underbelly of 1960s counterculture and threw the US in general—and the California glitterati in particular—into a state of fear. The murders involved manipulation, drug use, and cunning—all special talents of a charismatic career criminal like Charles Manson, whom Deputy DA Vincent Bugliosi famously denounced in his closing speech to the jury as "the dictatorial maharajah . . . of a tribe of bootlicking slaves."

---

[1] *Manson in His Own Words* by Charles Manson and Nuel Edmonds

[2] *The Life and Times of Charles Manson* by Jeff Guinn

[3] *24 Hours*, November 21, 2017—"Inside Charles Manson's Loveless Childhood"

[4] *Newsmax*, November 1, 2017—"Charles Manson as a Rock Star? Beach Boys' Dennis Wilson Was Believer Back in 1968"

[5] *The News Journal*, August 9, 2009—"Horror Haunts Free Manson Family Members"

[6] *The Life and Times of Charles Manson* by Jeff Guinn

[7] *Manson's Right-Hand Man Speaks Out* by Charles D. Watson

[8] *Charles Manson: Music Mayhem Murder* by Tommy Udo

[9] https://edition.cnn.com/2013/09/30/us/manson-family-murders-fast-facts/index.html

[10] *The New York Times*, February 10, 1971: "Miss Atkins Testifies She Killed Sharon Tate"

[11] *The Associated Press*, November 20, 2017—"For Many, Charles Manson Cult Killings Ended Era of Love"

[12] *Helter Skelter: Charles Manson, The Beatles and the Summer of '69* by Joseph Burns

The Symbionese Liberation Army

This extremist political cult made headlines around the world when it abducted newspaper heiress Patty Hearst. Controversy raged when images appeared of her toting a gun. Had she been forced to join in the SLA's slew of violent robberies, or was she a victim of brainwashing?

———————

"The only alternative to freedom is death

and the only way we can free ourselves from

the fascist dictatorship is by fighting, not with words

but with guns. I am a soldier of the people's army…"

Patty Hearst

———————

The Symbionese Liberation Army advocated revolution and vowed to overthrow the oppressive "establishment." This Californian terror group was an extreme manifestation of the civil unrest prevalent in the US during the early 1970s. Long before 1995's Oklahoma City bombing, the SLA was the embodiment of domestic terrorism.

The group was founded in Berkeley, California, in 1971 by Robyn Sue Steiner and Russell Little, who had first met at the University of Florida in Gainsville. Steiner was the daughter of middle-class parents in Miami; Little came from a working-class background in Pensacola, Florida. After moving to California, the pair became involved in radical politics and, according to an interview Steiner gave to *The New York Times* in 1979, they went up in the mountains for target practice.

Initially, the SLA was a loose band of radicals focused on prison reform, poverty, and race. They opposed what they perceived as the powerful influence of wealthy corporate interests over the government. The word "Symbionese" comes from the biological term "symbiosis," the interdependence of different species. The SLA defined the meaning as "a body of similar bodies and organisms living in deep and loving harmony and partnership in the best interests of all within the body."[1]

The SLA was born at a time when the US was experiencing a wave of protests and attacks by nationalist and ethnic terrorists, religious fanatics, and anti-Vietnam War organizations, many of which had grown out of 1960s countercultural movements. The SLA liked to think of themselves as modern-day Robin Hoods, stealing from wealthy capitalists to finance a revolution of the underprivileged.

This small group of middle- and upper-middle-class left-wing radicals believed that the re-election of Richard Nixon had ushered in a secret fascist coup.[2] The SLA's rhetoric drew on Marxist communism and the politics of South American revolutionaries, such as Ché Guevara. According to Les Payne, co-author of *The Life and Death of the SLA*, the group embraced Marxist French journalist Régis Debray's concept of "urban propaganda." This called for selective violence aimed at capturing the attention of the media. The SLA's symbol was a seven-headed cobra, and their media-grabbing slogan was "Death to the fascist insect that preys upon the life of the people." Their pamphlets asserted that the symbol signified "all universal forces of God and life."

In 1972, Donald DeFreeze, a convict in California's Vacaville Prison, met members of the SLA who were sitting in on a meeting of the prison group, the Black Cultural Association. In March 1973, DeFreeze escaped jail and made contact with the SLA. According to DeFreeze, revolutionary change could be led by small "vanguard groups" such as the SLA. The following year, Robyn Sue Steiner fled to England after DeFreeze hijacked leadership of the group and threatened to kill her. While DeFreeze wasn't particularly charismatic or intelligent, he managed to assemble a small band of followers.

On November 8, 1973, the SLA claimed responsibility for the murder of Marcus Foster, an African American school superintendent from Oakland, California. They ambushed Foster and his deputy, Robert Blackburn, as they left a school board meeting. It was later established that Foster and Blackburn had been shot with bullets tipped with cyanide; Foster died from his injuries, while Blackburn survived. The SLA sent a letter to a local news station claiming that they had targeted Foster because he represented a school system that perpetuated the values of the wealthy. They asserted that he wanted to impose a "political police force" by introducing identification cards into Oakland schools. Two months later, SLA members Joseph Remiro and Russell Little were arrested for the murder after a brief shootout with police. This act of terrorism reminded the nation that—despite the fact that US involvement in the Vietnam War was diminishing and the country was attempting to reclaim some of its lost innocence—extremist political turmoil was still lingering.

Patty Hearst was the 19-year-old daughter of Randolph Hearst, the chairman of the Hearst Corporation media conglomorate and the editor of the *San Francisco Examiner*. On February 4, 1974, she was relaxing with her fiancé, Steven Weed, in their apartment in Berkeley, California, when there was a knock at the door. When Weed opened the door, he was shoved aside as three armed SLA members—Donald DeFreeze, Angela Atwood, and William Wolfe—grabbed Hearst and carried her outside to their stolen Chevrolet.

The SLA claimed to have abducted Hearst in response to the arrests of Remiro and Little. She represented everything the SLA was against: she was a child of the establishment and was living comfortably off her family's vast wealth. The SLA maintained that the Hearst Corp. was the "corporate enemy of the people" and initially planned to use Hearst as a bargaining chip for the release of Remiro and Little. They then changed their minds and demanded that Hearst's parents, Randolph and Catherine, donate $4 million worth of food to the needy in California before the SLA would even consider negotiations to release their daughter. To the chagrin of the FBI, the Hearsts agreed to the SLA's demands. They developed the People in Need program, which saw millions of dollars' worth of food being thrown from the backs of trucks. Thousands of people showed up for the free food giveaway, triggering a riot and causing the Hearsts to balk at paying for more.

Over the forthcoming weeks, Hearst was kept locked in a closet-size room in an apartment near the University of San Francisco while her abductors conducted negotiations for her release. She was allegedly kept blindfolded while the SLA subjected her to Marxist readings and guerrilla warfare propaganda.

As her family, the media, and the public were still trying to come to terms with the kidnapping, they were shocked to discover that Hearst had transformed—or been transformed—from an innocent kidnapping victim into a gun-toting terrorist. On April 15, 1974, two months after her abduction, she was captured by surveillance cameras armed with an M-1 carbine during the SLA's robbery of the Hibernia Bank in San Francisco's Sunset District. The group got away with $10,000, but not before wounding two people, though not fatally. In a taped interview released to the media, Hearst—calling herself "Tania" after a comrade of Ché Guevara—announced that the idea she had been brainwashed was ridiculous. She denounced her fiancé Steven, who was campaigning for her release, as a "sexist pig," and went on to declare that "the only alternative to freedom is death and the only way we can free ourselves from this fascist dictatorship is by fighting, not with words but with guns. I am a soldier of the people's army . . ."[3]

The SLA proudly distributed photographs of Hearst, a.k.a. Tania, posing with a gun in front of the group's seven-headed snake symbol. Shortly afterward, DeFreeze, a.k.a. "Field Marshal Cinque," moved the group to Los Angeles. In mid-May 1974, Hearst and two other SLA members were caught shoplifting in Mel's Sporting Goods store in Inglewood, California. Hearst opened fire, and the three made a quick getaway. They kidnapped 17-year-old Thomas D. Matthews when they seized his van but later let him go unharmed. This run-in with the law led police to the SLA's hideout.

The search for Patty Hearst, one of the largest in the nation's history, culminated in a bloody shootout on May 17, 1974. Police had SLA members trapped inside their base in Los Angeles' South Central neighborhood. Following a 50-minute gun battle, during which it was estimated that more than 9,000 rounds of ammunition were discharged,[4] SWAT officers lobbed tear-gas grenades into the house. The grenades ignited an ammunition cache, and the house burst into flames. When the fire had burned out and the thick smoke had dissipated, six deceased SLA members—including DeFreeze, Angelina "General Gelina" Atwood, and William Wolfe, a man whom Hearst later described as "the gentlest, most beautiful man I have ever known"—were found huddled in the crawlspace. In a final act of defiance, DeFreeze had shot himself in the head. Hearst was not among the dead. She was holed up in a hotel near Disneyland watching the grim scenes unfold live on the television news.

The shootout closed the first chapter of the SLA's violent history but opened a second one. Although only three members of the SLA remained—Patty Hearst and William and Emily Harris—the deaths of their comrades had the effect of confirming their stance as revolutionaries. Before long, siblings Kathleen, Josephine, and Steven Soliah were recruited, along with James Kilgore. Over the ensuing months, the SLA survivors went on the run, criss-crossing the country in disguise, before settling in San Francisco, where they rebuilt the organization.

What the SLA lacked in numbers, it made up for in revolutionary zeal. "The SLA was back in business," Hearst recalled.[5] The members spent much of their time in San Francisco and Sacramento, staying in hotels and safe houses and supporting themselves by shoplifting food and stealing wallets and purses. In February 1975, their confidence restored, the group graduated to major crime, stealing $3,700 from the Guild Savings & Loan bank on the outskirts of Sacramento. The police did not link the bank robbery to the SLA, and the group quickly started planning another. Their next target was the Crocker National Bank, located in Carmichael, California. Only two SLA members had participated in the Guild Savings & Loan bank robbery—Kilgore and an ex-convict named Michael Bortin—but this time, more wanted to be involved.

On April 21, 1975, James Kilgore, Kathleen Soliah, Emily Harris, and Michael Bortin armed themselves with shotguns; to confuse the police, the two women dressed as men. The gang stormed the bank and ordered customers and employees alike to lie on the ground. In the confusion, Emily Harris shot and killed 42-year-old Myrna Lee Opsahl, a mother of four who was in the bank depositing church funds. Kathleen Soliah kicked a pregnant bank teller in the stomach, despite the fact that she wasn't resisting. The woman later lost her unborn child through a miscarriage. The group made off with $15,000 in their getaway cars, one of which was driven by Hearst.

The SLA's lust for violence was still unsatisfied and, in a perverse version of feminist thinking, the women of the group wanted to demonstrate their bomb-making skills. Hearst and Josephine Soliah took one bomb to San Francisco's Mission District, while Kathleen Soliah and new member Wendy Yoshimura took another to the Sunset District. They planted their bombs underneath patrol cars that were parked outside police stations; neither one exploded. After a test run in the wilderness, they decided to target the small city of Emeryville. On August 13, 1975, a bomb planted underneath a patrol car parked outside Emeryville police station exploded, destroying the car but harming nobody. The SLA sent a communiqué to the LAPD, warning, "The next bomb may be under the seat of your car." Several more bombs were planted throughout Los Angeles and Sacramento. While some detonated, nobody was injured.

In September, the FBI finally tracked down Patty Hearst, Wendy Yoshimura, Steven Soliah, and William and Emily Harris to a second-floor apartment in a neighborhood around 10 miles (16.1 km) from the San Francisco Bay area. None of them resisted arrest and, in stark contrast to the previous clash, there was no violence. The "romance of being a revolutionary lost its glitter," Hearst recalled.[6] James Kilgore, Kathleen Soliah, and Michael Bortin separately went on the run.

Emily and Bill Harris were convicted of kidnapping Hearst and sentenced to eight years in prison. Steven Soliah was tried on charges of robbing the Carmichael bank but acquitted in April 1976. Josephine Soliah was implicated in court records as having planted a bomb, but no charges were ever filed.

Meanwhile, lawyers Lee Bailey and J. Albert Johnson were hired by the Hearsts to defend their daughter against the armed robbery charges. They argued that their client had been brainwashed into joining the SLA and that following her arrest, "She just slowly freed herself from the brainwashing."[7]

When arrested, Patty Hearst gave a clenched-fist salute, and when she was being booked, she said that her occupation was "urban guerrilla."[8] However, by the time of her trial, she gave the distinct impression that she was a traumatized kidnap victim. Her dynamic public image as a radical revolutionary was no more; a subservient, "zombielike" woman now sat before the court. "In the closet, she became a revolutionary; in the jail cell, she became a Hearst," wrote Jeffrey Toobin in his 2016 book *American Heiress: The Wild Saga of the Kidnapping, Crimes and Trial of Patty Hearst.* Journalists jammed the US District Court for her trial. Hearst told the court that, during the first weeks of her captivity, she had been blindfolded, raped, and threatened. She said she only participated in the Hibernia Bank robbery because she feared for her life. Other members of the SLA strongly denied that Hearst had been abused in any way. "It's just lies created by Hearst's legal team to explain her behavior and it did not fly with her jury," Russell Little commented in 2005.[9] He also pointed out that the women of the group were all radical feminists and would never have condoned rape.

During the trial, Hearst pleaded the Fifth Amendment 42 times. "Her defense was physical duress, but it never squared with the facts," said US Attorney James L. Browning. On March 20, 1976, Patty Hearst was sentenced to seven years in prison for bank robbery. In the aftermath, her family launched a major media campaign to influence public opinion in her favor. In February 1979, President Carter took pity on the heiress and commuted her sentence by granting her executive clemency. Hearst was released from prison a free woman after serving just 22 months. Following her release, she wrote a memoir, *Every Secret Thing,* and co-authored the thriller *Murder at San Simeon*. She also appeared in a number of films, including 1990's *Cry Baby* as a suburban housewife. She went on to marry her bodyguard, Bernard Shaw, and on January 20, 2001, she was officially pardoned by President Bill Clinton.

Nevertheless, Hearst's time as an urban guerrilla in the SLA still causes controversy. According to a number of terrorism experts, brainwashing alone could not account for the depth of her complex conversion.[10] Whether Hearst was brainwashed or an eager accomplice in her own metamorphosis remains open to debate. Hearst almost certainly developed Stockholm Syndrome, a condition in which hostages come to strongly identify with their captors. The FBI has estimated that roughly 8 percent of kidnap victims show signs of Stockholm Syndrome, particularly those that are not mistreated or harmed.

The final chapter in the case unfolded with the arrests of former SLA members turned fugitives, who by now had settled into the self-same middle-class existence that they had once rebelled against. In 1999, the FBI finally caught up with Kathleen Soliah after a tip came in from somebody who recognized her on *America's Most Wanted*. Soliah—who now lived under the alias Sara Jane Olson—had been living quietly in Minnesota with her doctor husband and their three daughters. She pleaded guilty to possession of explosives with the intent to kill and was sentenced to two consecutive terms of 10 years to life. In 2002, first-degree murder charges were filed against Emily and William Harris, Sara Jane Olson, Michael Bortin, and James Kilgore. All were promptly apprehended, except for Kilgore. Several months later, he, too, was captured. The FBI tracked him down in Cape Town, South Africa, where he was working as a university lecturer. The following year, sentences were handed down. Emily Harris (now Montague) was sentenced to eight years; she claimed she shot Myrna Lee Opsahl accidentally when the safety on her gun slipped. However, Patty Hearst later said that she heard Harris justify the murder: "So what if she got shot? Her husband is a doctor. She's a bourgeois pig."

William Harris was sentenced to seven years, and Michael Bortin, James Kilgore, and Sara Jane Olson were sentenced to six years. All have since been released, including Russell Little, who was acquitted of the murder of Marcus Foster during a 1982 retrial. The only SLA member still behind bars is Joseph Remiro.

The Symbionese Liberation Army remains a prime example of the turbulence of early 1970s America. What began as youthful idealism soon transformed into terrorism. Unlike other radical groups of the 1960s and 1970s, such as the Black Panthers, the SLA weren't of great historical significance. Nevertheless, with the abduction of Patty Hearst, this group of mainly middle-class, well-educated urban guerrillas secured their notoriety in the annals of American crime.

---

[1] *The Petaluma Argus-Courier*, February 13, 1974—"Letter, Tapes Outline Policy of Symbionese Army"

[2] *Guerrilla: The Taking of Patty Hearst* by Robert Stone

[3] *American Heiress: The Kidnapping, Crimes and Trial of Patty Hearst* by Jeffrey Toobin

[4] *The San Francisco Chronicle*, May 18, 1974—"Shootout in L.A."

[5] *The News-Gazette*, February 9, 2014—"In Plain Sight"

[6] *Every Secret Thing* by Patricia Hearst

[7] *San Francisco Chronicle*, February 4, 1999—"The Kidnapping that Gripped the Nation"

[8] *Patty's Got a Gun: Patricia Hearst in 1970s America* by William Graebner

[9] *The Observer*, May 29, 2005—"Barmy Army"

[10] *The Chicago Tribune*, August 21, 1988—"Patricia Shaw Hearst"

Synanon

The story of Synanon is a tale of good intentions betrayed. Its charismatic leader's neuroses and lust for power turned a revolutionary therapeutic program for drug addiction into a dark, disturbing cult associated with hit lists, violent acts, sexual oppression, and brainwashing.

"Today is the first day of the rest of your life."

Charles Dederich

Synanon was founded in Santa Monica, California, in 1958 by Charles E. "Chuck" Dederich using just one week's state unemployment benefit of $33. Dederich was born in Toledo, Ohio, on March 22, 1913. When he was just 4 years old, his alcoholic father died in a car accident. He was raised by his mother as a devout Roman Catholic, but when he turned 14, he read H. G. Wells' *The Outline of History* and claimed he became a militant atheist "almost overnight."[1]

As an adult, Dederich subsequently developed a drinking problem and flunked out of California's prestigious Notre Dame University. By the late 1950s, Dederich's alcohol dependency had spiraled out of control. He had a failed business career and two broken marriages behind him when he made his way to California. After finally beating his alcohol addiction with the help of Alcoholics Anonymous, Dederich became a staunch advocate for the organization. However, he was dismayed that it did not offer support to those addicted to other substances. After participating in a controlled LSD experiment conducted on alcoholics at the University of California, which he later referred to as "the most important single experience in my entire life,"[2] Dederich founded Synanon, the first-ever drug rehabilitation center. The name "Synanon" came from a confused drug addict who stumbled over the words "symposium" and "seminar."

Members lived together in a commune and dealt with their addictions under Dederich's tough-love leadership. Before Synanon was properly established, Dederich ran into legal trouble; Santa Monica city officials claimed that he was operating a hospital in a residential zone. An ensuing legal battle ended with Dederich serving 25 days in jail. This episode had the effect of rallying Dederich supporters and, most importantly, brought Synanon much-needed publicity. Drug addicts in search of succor flocked to California. When the membership became too large for Dederich's apartment, he rented a storefront in Ocean Park, Santa Monica, where he conducted his meetings and also offered lodgings.

Synanon was a communitarian scheme modeled on the 12-step Alcoholics Anonymous program. Rules were simple: no alcohol, no drugs, and no physical violence. Synanon followed a philosophy of individual responsibility by forcing individuals into a position where their actions were made public and they were therefore forced to defend themselves or change their behavior. The cornerstone of the rehabilitation program was a complex group therapy known as the "Synanon game." This often brutal and confrontational procedure, subsequently known as "Attack therapy," was a free-form encounter session where Synanon members sat in a circle and spoke freely about their issues. There was no limit to what could be said, and prolonged, aggressive verbal attacks were commonplace. Those living at Synanon were required to get menial jobs, such as working in a gas station or selling pencils. The purpose was to instill a work ethic in the troubled souls that called Synanon home.

During the 1960s, Synanon's work was acclaimed as a way to get drug addicts off the street, rehabilitated, and reintegrated into the real world. In 1965, *Synanon,* starring Chuck Connors and Stella Stevens, a hard-hitting, mainstream Hollywood movie celebrating the organization, was released. The role of Charles Dederich was played by the well-known character actor Edmond O'Brien. Charles Dederich claimed that Synanon's recovery rates were between 80 to 100 percent. However, these figures were never confirmed by outside sources.

Synanon underwent a drastic change in 1968, when Dederich decided to scrap the goal of "graduation" after two or three years. Dederich decided that the outside world was corrupt and that the only way to ensure that Synanon members remained cured was to keep them confined at Synanon. Turning away from its original purpose—rehabilitating drug addicts—Synanon became a communal social experiment and a lifelong commitment. Synanon thus became an alternative society, from birth to death, for anybody who wished to join. Dederich was credited with coining the famous quote, "Today is the first day of the rest of your life." The concept of communal life was popular at the time, and numerous well-to-do nonaddicts begged to join. They were known as "Squares" or "Lifestylers." Lifestylers brought various managerial talents to Synanon and were expected to sell everything they owned and turn the proceeds over to it. The organization became a considerable economic and social presence in California, attracting the favorable attention of numerous celebrities, including Jane Fonda, Charlton Heston, Leonard Nimoy, Timothy Leary, artist Buckminster Fuller, as well as leading politicians.

As Synanon's fame grew, donations started to roll in. Dorothy Salant Garrett, the cousin by marriage of CBS executive Richard Salant, contributed more than $1 million. Synanon rapidly went from a struggling nonprofit charity to a sprawling multi-million-dollar organization. A new branch opened in Detroit, Michigan, and built up a solid clientele of Michigan businesses. During its peak, Synanon had real estate in Santa Monica, Los Angeles, San Diego, San Francisco, Tomales Bay, Reno, Detroit, New York City, and Puerto Rico.

In addition, Synanon members produced embossed promotional products such as pens, coffee mugs, and keychains. Although Synanon had stepped away from being a drug rehabilitation facility, it continued to attract businesses to make donations by instructing members to tug at heartstrings with emotional stories of how Synanon had helped them overcome their addiction. Synanon's sales pitch was that donations would help keep drug addicts off the streets, help them lead productive lives, and also lower crime rates. Companies that donated to Synanon included Chrysler Corp., Dow Chemical, and Upjohn.

In 1972, despite the fact that Synanon had no license as a juvenile care home, the Michigan Legislature spent $300,000 to send drug-addicted teenagers to live at Synanon in California. The state's main branch was in the scenic mountain area of Tomales Bay, West Marin; it would grow into a 3,300-acre (1,335.5-hectare) complex complete with houses, dormitories, warehouses, meeting halls, and its own airstrip. Synanon was not open to inspection by state health officials; nevertheless, the juvenile justice system and exasperated parents sent delinquent juveniles from the ages of 9 to 18 there. Synanon responded to this influx of children by forming the "punk squad," which was billed as a program to help "cure" these "character-disordered" children. Those enrolled in the punk squad had to get up at 4 a.m. to take part in a grueling regime that included marching, running, and strenuous exercise.

The program failed miserably, and more than 75 percent of the troubled teenagers either demanded to leave Synanon or ran away. Many children and teenagers sent to Synanon complained that they had been mistreated and abused, but these claims were quietly forgotten about by the authorities, along with the aborted program.[3]

Despite this setback, Synanon maintained a positive public profile until the mid-1970s, when Dederich proclaimed that Synanon was now a religion, with himself as the "charismatic wizard-leader."[4] Its classification as a religion meant that Synanon was exempt from charitable socialization laws, which regulate charities and their donations. Synanon could now operate unchecked, and before long, it was worth $30 million and owned vast tracts of real estate across the United States, as well as hundreds of vehicles, planes, and boats. Dederich's obsessive edicts included forcing male followers to shave their heads and undergo vasectomies to prevent overpopulation. In another bid to prevent overpopulation, Dederich ordered five pregnant women to have abortions. "Having an abortion is like squeezing a boil, nothing more," Dederich announced. One woman refused to terminate her pregnancy and was forced to leave with her husband. When Dederich stopped smoking, he ordered his followers to stop smoking. When Dederich went on a diet, he ordered his followers to go on a diet. When Dederich began to wear overalls, he ordered his followers to wear overalls. In time, Synanon members became mirror images of their increasingly eccentric leader.

As Synanon morphed into an insular cult, it also grew more violent. During one session of the "Synanon game" in 1973, Charles Dederich became so enraged at another participant that he poured root beer over her head. To the outside world, this might seem an innocuous incident. However, it signaled the start of the violence at Synanon.

By the mid-1970s, Synanon was being widely criticized. According to former members, its techniques, such as the "Synanon game," were being used to undermine participants' self-confidence to the point that they became totally dependent on the cult. The game was simply a brainwashing tool. Loyalty to Synanon was all-important, gaining precedence over family relationships. The famous Eagles song "Hotel California" was reportedly inspired by the Synanon program, which "you can never leave."

At the same time, Dederich became increasingly paranoid and began to plan elaborate attacks on those he perceived as enemies. When the media ran exposés on the goings-on at Synanon, Dederich convinced his followers that they were under attack by the government itself. He gave orders to stockpile guns and ammunition and formed a paramilitary force he called the Imperial Marines that consisted of men trained in martial arts and military survival. The Imperial Marines compiled a "hit list" of people perceived as enemies of Synanon, including former Synanon president Jack Hurst and Phil Ritter, a one-time Synanon member who had tried to get his young daughter out of the cult. Dederich explained this move as follows: "If you misbehave in my house I'll have you . . . beat up or something, you see? Literally. What the hell's the matter with that? We think it's great."

Dederich's megalomania and paranoia increased when his third wife, Betty, died in 1977. "When she went, there were no restraints," recalled one Synanon member.[5] For weeks, Dederich was inconsolable, then one day, he snapped out of it. He chose a new wife from a list of potential partners and then ordered that all married members of Synanon should divorce and take new partners. Those who declined—including Dedrich's own brother—were forced to leave or subjected to verbal attacks to make them comply.

After Charles Dederich ordered couples to separate and take new partners, he held "separation ceremonies." During the ceremony, women were auctioned to the highest bidder.

By the late-70s, ex-members traumatized by their physically and emotionally grueling experiences at Synanon began to tell stories of mental and physical abuse. Tracy Bogard, 32, blamed the group for stripping her of her identity and manipulating her into obeying the whims of Synanon's leadership.[6] A 19-year-old man who had attempted to escape Synanon said that he was captured and badly beaten. He said the beating was recorded and then played back that night on "the wire"—Synanon's internal radio station—as a grim warning to others.

A teenage boy, Joey Butler, recalled that he was slapped, kicked, and pinned against a wall for not wearing a required neckerchief. Butler wasn't at Synanon for drug rehabilitation or juvenile delinquency: He was simply the son of Synanon parents. The children of Synanon experienced brutal punishments. Butler recalled that on one occasion, a 10-year-old girl didn't attend her aerobics class. He said that a Synanon leader subsequently came into the dormitory where the young girl was sleeping and kicked her over and over again in the back. On another occasion, a group of children who attempted to run away from Synanon were pushed into a ditch and beaten. One 15-year-old girl who lived at Synanon with her mother and two sisters filed a declaration with a Los Angeles court contending that she was harshly disciplined. "I was always being hit. If I didn't run in basic training, I was hit. If I did an exercise wrong, I was hit," she said. The same girl recollected how three boys were caught trying to run away. "Two of them were slammed against a metal building over and over . . . The third boy was punched in the stomach." Violent punishments at Synanon were so prevalent that the regular five o'clock meetings were nicknamed "Five O'Clock Beatings" by the children. Ritual humiliation was also common. Butler recalled an occasion when the children, who were sleeping on the beach as part of an exercise regimen, were all awoken and ordered to smear mud on a boy who had allegedly misbehaved.

Synanon responded to the negative press reports by arguing that the group had taken in society's rejects, not all of whom were capable of adapting to the prescribed therapy. Synanon admitted they used corporal punishment on children in the punk squad but contended that their parents gave permission. "We do what any proper American family would do. If some kid acts out in a way that's offensive to me, I'm going to knock him on his ass," explained Synanon attorney Dan Garrett.

Synanon's past success as a drug-rehabilitation program initially prevailed over negative reports such as these, but eventually it was difficult to deny its cultlike activities and stories of abuse. An independent "watchdog," the Marin County Civil Grand Jury, started looking into claims of child abuse, while the State Health Department investigated how an unlicensed organization such as Synanon came to accept so many juveniles into its care. Synanon responded by stating it was exempt from licensing.

In 1975, three members of Synanon assaulted a Marin County rancher. Another rancher was pistol-whipped. In Santa Monica, members of Synanon assaulted two black couples who had parked their car at a Synanon building.

During the 1970s, Synanon sued a number of organizations that had made negative statements about the cult. Synanon sued KGO-TV for slander, claiming that a series of broadcasts in 1978 that mentioned Synanon's purchase of guns implied that it was a terrorist group. In 1982, American Broadcasting Companies, who owned KGO, paid Synanon $1.2 million to drop the lawsuit.

Synanon also sued the *San Francisco Examiner* for calling the cult the "Racket of the Century." The newspaper paid $600,000 and ran a front-page apology. In 1981, Charles Dederich filed a lawsuit against *Readers Digest* and David MacDonald for the article "The Little Paper that Dared," which chronicled how *The Point Reyes Light* newspaper won a 1979 Pulitzer Prize for a series exposing the cult. Dederich's libel suit was dismissed by a judge for lack of evidence that the article was written in malice.

Charles Dederich was intensely paranoid that there was a media conspiracy against Synanon. He went to great lengths to thwart media coverage of the cult. A number of news directors became so worried about their employees' welfare that they hired bodyguards and even lawyers to accompany them on stories about Synanon. In 1977, *Time* magazine referred to Synanon as a "kooky cult," and reporters were threatened. "I don't know what these people might do. I don't know what action they might take against the people responsible, their wives, their children . . . Bombs could be thrown into odd places, into the homes of some of the clowns who occupy high places in the *Time* organization," threatened Charles Dederich to a television reporter.[7] In 1978, NBC ran an exposé on Synanon. Afterward, they received hundreds of letters from members of Synanon, who threatened them with physical violence.

A 1978 report of the Marin County Grand Jury called Synanon's nonprofit status into question, claiming that top executives received substantial salaries and retirement bonuses. (In 1977, Dederich himself had been awarded a $500,000 retirement bonus.) In August 1978, the State Board of Equalization stripped Synanon of its property tax exemptions on almost $10 million worth of property after they determined that Synanon could no longer prove its vast holdings were intended exclusively for rehabilitation.

In October the following year, Synanon's downfall was truly set in motion when Dederich ordered the murder of Pacific Palisades lawyer Paul Morantz. He had represented a woman who had been held against her will at Synanon and won a $300,000 settlement against the cult. Two of Dederich's acolytes, Lance Keaton and Joe Musico, deposited a 4-ft-6-in (1.8-m) rattlesnake in Morantz's mailbox. When Morantz went to retrieve his mail, the snake bit him. Morantz was hospitalized for six days but survived. The attack led to an investigation of Synanon and a raid on the commune, during which officers discovered a tape in which Dederich was heard to say, "I'm quite willing to break some lawyer's legs, and then tell him, 'Next time, I'm going to break your wife's legs, and then we are going to cut your kid's ear off. That is the end of that lawyer. That is a very satisfactory, humane way of transmitting information. I really do want an ear in a glass of alcohol on my desk.'"[8]

The subsequent arrests of Dederich (who was found in an alcoholic stupor and had to be carried to jail on a stretcher), Keaton, and Musico finally revealed the cult's criminality. Keaton and Musico pleaded no contest to charges of assault and conspiracy to commit murder. Dederich also pleaded no contest and was sentenced to probation and a $10,000 fine. He was also forced to step down from leading Synanon, the organization he had founded. Synanon's prominence and prestige rapidly declined. The snake incident and a steady stream of exposés prompted further investigations and, in 1991, the Internal Revenue Service revoked Synanon's tax-exempt status and ordered it to pay $17 million. Synanon was discredited and disbanded shortly thereafter. In 1997, Charles Dederich died of cardiovascular failure in Visalia, California, finally closing the door on the cult.

When Synanon was founded, Charles Dederich's timing could not have been better. America was suffering from an opiate epidemic, and psychiatrists claimed that the addiction was untreatable. Over a 20-year span, it was estimated that 15,000 to 20,000 people lived in Synanon communities. Synanon was praised for its innovative techniques in treating drug addiction, and Dederich's approach to the rehabilitation of drug addicts—including famous jazz musicians Joe Pass and Art Pepper—became a prototype for drug recovery all over the world. Synanon was lavished with praise by the mainstream press, and Dederich was lauded for saving drug addicts' lives. But as Synanon shifted focus from rehabilitation to a communal lifestyle, Dederich's megalomania led to its collapse, leading it to be referred to by Matt Novak, author of *The Man Who Fought the Synanon Cult and Won* as one of the "most dangerous and violent cults America has ever seen."[9]

---

[1] *From Miracle to Madness: The True Story of Charles Dederich and Synanon* by Paul Morantz

[2] *Los Angeles Magazine*, April 23, 2018—"The Story of This Drug Rehab-Turned-Violent Cult Is Wild, Wild Country-Caliber Bizarre"

[3] *The Rise and Fall of Synanon: A California Utopia* by Rod A. Janzen

[4] *The Los Angeles Times*, October 17, 2001—"The Evolution and Devolution of a Self-Help Group"

[5] *Chicago Tribune*, December 3, 1978—"With Each New Life Saved, Synanon's Fame Grew"

[6] *Detroit Free Press*, November 1, 1979—"Synanon Cult Reports Mar Claims of Cure"

[7] *Escape from Utopia: My Ten Years in Synanon* by William F. Olin

[8] *The Indianapolis Star*, December 24, 1978—"Synanon Members Disillusioned"

[9] *The Man Who Fought the Synanon Cult and Won* by Matt Novak

Peoples Temple

Praised for championing the poor and civil rights in 1970s San Francisco, the Reverend Jim Jones dreamed of creating a "socialist paradise" for his Peoples Temple. A few years later, the world looked on in horror as more than 900 of his idealistic followers lay dead in the Guyanese jungle.

"You're gonna help yourself, or you'll get no help! There's only one hope of glory; that's within you!"

Reverend Jim Jones

Jonestown, the agricultural camp of the Peoples Temple, was nestled in the lush jungles of northwestern Guyana. Families lived in cottages or dorms, raised their own livestock, and grew their own food. To outsiders, Jonestown seemed like a utopian paradise. However, behind its peaceful façade lurked deep, dark tensions and stresses that would erupt into intimidation, violence, terror, and, ultimately, mass murder.

On November 18, 1978, the news reverberated around the globe that a well-known Bay Area congressman investigating Peoples Temple had been shot dead. Furthermore, the cult's leader, the Rev. Jim Jones, had ordered the mass murder-cum-suicide of hundreds of his loyal followers. Reports showing vats of cyanide-laced fruit punch surrounded by the bodies of men, women, and children—some of whom were locked in a final embrace—flashed across television screens. As viewers gazed open-mouthed in horror, one question was foremost in their minds: How, in the modern world, could something like this happen? Many of the answers lay in the charismatic but deranged personality of the Peoples Temple founder and leader.

The Rev. Jim Jones was born James Warren Jones on May 13, 1931.

His family lived in a rundown home near railroad tracks in the rural farming town of Crete, Indiana, on the fringes of the US's Bible Belt. His father, James Thurman Jones, had been badly affected by fighting in the trenches during World War I. Some neighbors speculated that he had been exposed to mustard gas; others dismissed him as an alcoholic. Jones' father was also a virulent racist, and despised his son for making friends with local black children. Jones' mother, Lynetta Putnam, was 15 years younger than her husband and had been married once before. She did housekeeping and factory work in Richmond, Indiana, while James worked as a railroad section hand. As a young boy, Jones was often sent outside with a packed lunch. He would wander around the neighborhood on his own and sometimes knock on a neighbor's door and ask to be let in. "My mom was in the kitchen having coffee one day, and there was this little kid at the door with his sack lunch," recollected a neighbor, Phyllis Wilmore.[1]

In high school, Jones tended to hang around with kids a few years younger than him. They were easier to boss around and manipulate. He enjoyed collecting and killing small animals and conducting funerals for them. He also often pretended he was Hitler and would lecture friends about sex. Even at a young age, influenced by the prevailing fundamentalist Protestantism of his community, Jones had a need to dominate and to proselytize. He would assemble a congregation of young people in a loft above a garage and preach sermons laced with hellfire and damnation.

By the age of 16, Jones was working as a hospital porter and married to a student nurse five years older than him named Marceline Baldwin, whom he met while working part-time as an orderly in Reid Memorial Hospital, Richmond. They married in 1949, the year Jones graduated from high school. The young couple enrolled at Indiana University, where he studied education and she studied nursing education. Ambitions to become a doctor led him to briefly enroll at Indiana University. Aged 21, Jones dropped out to become a student minister, seeking converts for a Methodist church. However his passionate, hectoring preaching style and strong views on civil rights made him an uneasy fit. He renounced the Methodists because the church refused to accommodate the black converts he brought them.

In 1956, Jones finally created a platform for his evangelical impulses, founding Peoples Temple, an integrated church combining religion and socialist politics, in Indianapolis. He drew large, interracial crowds of mainly poor people who felt "left-behind" or alienated by society—much like himself. Jones conducted "miracle healings," and preached about civil rights and equality.[2] His sermons combined elements of Leninism, Christianity, and Buddhism. Jones' followers hung on his every word; he was their messiah. His wife commented in a 1977 interview in *The New York Times*: "Jim has used religion to try to get some people out of the opiate of religion." She recalled how he slammed a Bible on the table yelling: "Marcie, I've got to destroy this paper idol!" In one sermon, Jones said, "You're gonna help yourself, or you'll get no help! There's only one hope of glory; that's within you! Nobody's gonna come out of the sky! There's no heaven up there! We'll have to make heaven down here!"[3]

After Jones read an article in *Esquire* magazine that claimed that Mendocino County, California, was one of "The Best Places to Survive a Nuclear Attack,"[3] he and the most loyal members of his flock relocated to Mendocino's largest city, Ukiah, in 1965. However, Jones had another, more practical, reason for moving: Under California's liberal welfare policies at the time, poor Temple members would qualify for government aid, which could be handed over to Jones. In Redwood Valley, just 8 miles (13 km) north of Ukiah, Jones set up a sprawling new church.

Jones was viewed as somewhat eccentric by local people in Redwood Valley, but he quickly gained a positive reputation. Peoples Temple accepted members from all backgrounds and races and, before long, had grown from a ministry based on dubious faith healing to one involved in praiseworthy social and racial justice programs. Jones' following included a number of black Americans who were disillusioned with the authorities' attitude to race relations. When Temple members weren't preaching about racial equality and economic justice, they would be visiting the sick, feeding the homeless, and caring for the elderly. Jones opened up a soup kitchen, a nursing home, a clothing pantry and also a service to help young people in poor neighborhoods find work. He even persuaded some theaters and restaurants to change their racially discriminatory practices. As the political influence and reach of Peoples Temple grew, Jones opened new branches in Los Angeles and San Francisco, finally relocating Temple headquarters to a building on Geary Boulevard, San Francisco, California. Jones' profile was rising rapidly and he cultivated connections with San Francisco's political elite. He was hailed as a blend of Martin Luther King, Einstein, and Mao by 41st Mayor of San Francisco Willie Brown. He was also commended for his activism by California Governor Jerry Brown, and—as late as April 1977—by the First Lady herself, Rosalynn Carter.

The sense of community and acceptance that Peoples Temple appeared to offer enticed many idealistic souls to join. However, the organization also had its dark side. Ex-members claimed that Jones exploited racial fears and instilled group paranoia, offering himself and Peoples Temple as the only possible salvation. Some followers began to grow disillusioned with—or even frightened of—Jones, who was becoming increasingly paranoid. He would ramble on for hours about spying and persecution by the CIA and FBI, about a coming fascist leader who would take over America, and the certainty of nuclear holocaust. Lurid tales began to emerge of members—adults and children alike—being routinely beaten for violating the Temple's strict rules. Defectors from the church came forward to say that they had been pressured to sign over their homes and life savings, leaving them penniless and utterly dependent on the church.

Even more disturbing were tales that Jones ruled the most intimate aspects of his followers' lives, demanding that some be celibate and assigning sexual partners to others. To his most fanatical followers, Jones was God, and as God, he was allowed to be intimate with whomever he pleased, regardless of age or gender. Jones even judged the loyalty of male members by testing whether they were willing to be sodomized by him. Defectors contended that Peoples Temple was a dangerous cult masquerading as a church and that they feared for their lives.

These rumors were soon picked up by local journalists. Jones responded to their inquiries with lawsuit threats, claiming religious oppression.[4] As Jones became increasingly afraid of defections, he urged followers to spy on each other and report back if they discovered a member was thinking of leaving. His use of spies and informants, combined with his policy of breaking up families and encouraging extra-marital relationships, left Temple members feeling as if they had only one loyalty—to Jones himself.

In 1974, Jones signed a 25-year lease for 3,852 acres of land in the Guyanese jungle, near the Venezuelan border; he had, for some time, viewed the US as corrupt and evil and had convinced himself that the country was doomed. Jones was seeking to create his own socialist state, far away from the prying eyes of police, reporters, and politicians, all of whom he believed were persecuting him. Jones had visited Guyana in the 1960s while working as a missionary in Belo Horizonte, Brazil, and found the socialist regime sympathetic. A group of Temple members worked tirelessly in the humid Guyanese heat to develop the new agricultural camp, to be named Jonestown. They built roads and wooden buildings, including cottages, dorms, a dining facility, a school, and medical facilities. They raised livestock and grew fruit and vegetables, including pineapple, cassava and eddoes. "We built a community out of nothing in four years," recalled Mike Touchette, one of the Temple members who helped develop Jonestown. "Being in Jonestown before Jim got there was the best thing in my life."[5]

Conditions in Jonestown worsened dramatically following Jones' arrival. In particular, previously plentiful food became scarce and medicines—essential in the jungle environment—were in increasingly short supply. The first "White Night" mass suicide rehearsal took place on January 1, 1976. Followers voluntarily took poison to prove their loyalty to Jones and Peoples Temple. The mixture turned out to be harmless.

On August 1, 1977, *New West* magazine, based in Los Angeles, ran an exposé that unmasked the "real" Jim Jones. The piece revealed the physical, emotional, and sexual abuse some Temple members had endured, drawing on first-hand accounts from 30 former members. Michael Cartmell, who was married to one of Jones' daughters until he escaped the cult, told of one particularly brutal beating in which a child "was paddled 150 times on his buttocks," adding that "the kid passed out from it."[6] Other members revealed that they had been forced to sign false confessions of crimes, which Jones would use as blackmail material if they ever tried to leave. The article also detailed how *New West* had received a barrage of communications from Temple supporters urging it to halt its investigation, including a phone call from California's Lieutenant Governor Mervyn Dymally—a staunch defender of Peoples Temple—and a letter from the famous gay rights activist Harvey Milk. The night before the story ran, Jones was tipped off about the contents. Realizing that it would threaten his reputation and lead to an investigation by the authorities, Jones told his followers that they were under attack by outside forces and that they should be ready to die for their beliefs. He ordered a mass exodus to Jonestown in Guyana and almost 1,000 Temple members obeyed. They arrived in Jonestown just before the magazine hit the shelves.

The Temple members who followed Jones to his socialist promised land soon discovered that Jonestown was no utopian safe haven. They found themselves cut off from civilization—the nearest small town was Port Kaituma, some 7 miles (11 km) away through dense jungle. New arrivals were met by a Greeting Committee and their passports and personal belongings were confiscated. Any prescription medicines they were carrying were seized by armed guards for Jones' personal use. By now, Jones was addicted to a plethora of drugs, including Valium, barbiturates, speed and LSD, all of which fueled his paranoid delusions. His drug abuse and deteriorating mental state made him increasingly erratic, and he demanded unquestioning loyalty and obedience from his followers.

Meanwhile, back in the US, the *New West* article about Jones and the activities of Peoples Temple had created quite a stir, and the media was working on follow-up stories, interviewing Temple members who had stayed behind and family members of those in Jonestown.

Then, in June 1978, Deborah Layton, the sister of one of Jones' most trusted lieutenants, Larry Layton, escaped from Guyana while on an official trip to the capital Georgetown, 150 miles (240 km) away. She declared that Jonestown was an armed camp and that Jones was regularly staging "White Night" suicide drills in the middle of the night in case the outside world should invade Jonestown.[7] In November, US Congressman Leo Ryan led a delegation to investigate claims of abuse and claims that Temple members were being held against their will. He arrived in Jonestown on November 18, 1978, landing at Port Kaituma airstrip with a party of journalists from San Francisco newspapers and the *Washington Post* as well as an NBC film crew. To mark his arrival, Peoples Temple held an enthusiastic concert, while smiling members recited carefully scripted comments about how Jonestown was the best thing that had ever happened to them. Tragically, within hours, almost every last one of them would be dead.

This warm welcome initially impressed Ryan, but events took a sinister turn when a Temple member, Monica Bagby, slipped Ryan a note saying that 16 Temple members wanted to return to the United States with Ryan. Ryan's decision to respond to these wishes would prove to be the catalyst for the ensuing carnage. Jones was convinced that Ryan would instigate a process to dismantle all that Jones had built. Jones had dreamed up Jonestown and he was determined that he—and only he—would destroy it. As Ryan and his entourage, as well as a party of "defectors," got ready to board two small aircraft at Port Kaituma airstrip, they were ambushed by a squad of armed enforcers from Peoples Temple known as the "Red Brigade," who had been dispatched by Jones. In addition, among the Peoples Temple defectors on one of the planes was Jones' enforcer Larry Layton, who started shooting, wounding two people.

The gunfire from the Red Brigade killed Ryan, San *Francisco Examiner* photographer Greg Robinson, NBC newsman Don Harris, NBC cameraman Bob Brown, and Patricia Parks, a member of the Temple who was leaving with the crew. Ten others were wounded; five of the party escaped to Port Kaituma in the smaller of the two planes.

Back in Jonestown, an even greater horror was unfolding. Loud-speakers ordered members to the dining room, where Jones—claiming that the community was about to be attacked by US-backed forces—ordered "revolutionary suicide protesting the conditions of an inhumane world." He brought in a vat filled with a fruit-flavored concoction laced with Valium and cyanide and ordered Temple members to "die with dignity." Some were forced to drink by armed guards of the Jonestown security force, while others willingly drank the deadly mixture, even pouring it into the mouths of their sobbing children. "I look at all the babies and think they deserve to live," said one defiant member. Her words fell on deaf ears. Within hours, 909 more people, including 267 babies and children, were dead.

Only 36 members of Peoples Temple who were in Jonestown on the day of the massacre survived. One disillusioned follower, Hyacinth Thrash, 76, realized what was happening and hid underneath her bed. Another, Grover Davis, 79, who was hearing-impaired, didn't hear the announcement. Eleven Temple members managed to escape into the jungle before the mass murder-suicide began. All but one of the defectors who planned to leave with Congressman Leo Ryan survived the attack, but several were seriously wounded. A few other survivors were on official Peoples Temple trips elsewhere at the time.

Rev. Jim Jones' wife, Marceline, 51, died in Jonestown, along with their adopted daughter, Agnes Jones, 36, and adopted son,

Lew Eric Jones, 22. Their natural son, Stephan Gandhi Jones, 19 and two adopted sons, Jim Jones Jr. and Tim Tupper Jones,17 and 19, escaped death because, as members of the Jonestown basketball team, they were in Georgetown participating in a tournament. Jones' other adopted daughter, Suzanne, 26, survived because, to her father's chagrin, she had rejected the Temple's influence and was safe in California.

In addition to the deaths in Jonestown, four other members who were in the Temple's Georgetown headquarters also committed suicide. Sharon Amos received radio messages from Jonestown instructing them all to commit suicide. Sharon slashed the throats of two of her children, Christa, 11, and Martin, 10. Her daughter, Liane, 21, then helped Sharon die before turning the knife on herself. This took the death toll to 918. Most were never legally identified and many bore signs that they did not go to their deaths willingly.

Unwilling to succumb to cyanide poisoning's painful death, Jones shot himself in the head. Investigators later found a chilling 43-minute tape on which he could be heard encouraging Temple members to have their children drink the cyanide-laced punch before drinking it themselves. He admonishes those who can be heard in the background screaming and crying.

Jones also left behind a note declaring that more than $7 million in Temple assets should be donated to the USSR. Where the money truly went is unknown, even today.

For many years, the Jonestown massacre represented the largest loss of American civilian lives—it was surpassed by the 9/11 Twin Towers terror attack. As the news broke and horrifying images of hundreds of lifeless bodies flashed around the world, many people were persuaded that those who followed Rev. Jim Jones to Guyana must have been naïve and gullible. This may have been true, but the cult was also successful because Jones mercilessly took advantage of desires shared by many Americans—a longing for a purpose, a family, racial equality, and economic opportunity. "They were not fools in any sense," confirmed James S. Gordon, a psychiatrist who interviewed 20 survivors of the cult. "They believed in many of the ideals that ordinary Americans share." Jones' followers joined Peoples Temple with the best of intentions, but—along with numerous politicians and, initially, the press—were manipulated by Jones' undeniably charismatic, super-confident personality. The grim exploits of Rev. Jim Jones and his Peoples Temple have become the subject of numerous books and documentaries, including *Jonestown: the Life and Death of Peoples Temple* (2006), and *Jonestown: Terror in the Jungle* (2018). The horrific scenes that unfolded in Jonestown on that fateful day stand as the starkest of warnings of the damage modern-day cults may do to their adherents.

----

[1] *San Francisco Chronicle*, November 18, 2003—"Jonestown—25 Years Later"

[2] *The Press Democrat*, November 18, 1998—"Temple Fading Into History"

[3] *Jonestown: The Life and Death of Peoples Temple* (2006)

[4] *The Mercury News*, November 16, 1998—"Horror, Then Hope 20 Years After Peoples Temple Tragedy"

[5] *Associated Press*, November 14, 2018—"Young Jonestown Survivors Built New Lives Amid Grief, Scorn"

[6] *The Chicago Tribune*, November 26, 1978—"'Reincarnated Christ' Turns Out To Be The Devil"

[7] *The Press Democrat*, November 15, 1998—"Led To Darkness"

The Fall River Cult

Fall River, Massachusetts, attracted national attention in the late 1970s when three young sex workers were brutally murdered. Was it the work of a devil-worshipping cult? As "satanic panic" gripped the US, worried parents wondered: Was the nation's youth becoming obsessed with the occult?

"A lot of these people we talked to were heavy drug users and we're wondering whether this cult exists in their minds or is it a real thing."

Capt. Ronald Andrade,

Fall River Police Department

On October 13, 1979, two early-morning joggers discovered the body of Doreen Levesque, a 17-year-old habitual runaway, beneath the bleachers of a sports field behind the Diman Regional Vocational Technical High School in Fall River. Levesque had been beaten to death with a rock. Cause of death was a massive hemorrhage to the head. She had also been stabbed several times in the head and sexually assaulted. When she was discovered, she was lying face down in a pool of blood and her ankles and wrists had been tied with twine and fishing line. She was nude except for a blue shirt; the rest of her clothing was discovered nearby. Also near her body was a rock with a tooth and hair stuck to it. It was estimated that she had been murdered at around 2 a.m. and had either walked or been carried to the spot where she was killed—a fence around the field made it impossible for a vehicle to have transported her there. It was soon discovered that Levesque was a sex worker, predominantly working the Bedford Street area, and investigators initially assumed that she had been killed by a client.

Around a month later, Andy Maltias, a 43-year-old divorced father of three, visited the Fall River police station to file a missing persons report for Barbara Raposa, 19, his girlfriend and the mother of one of his children. Like Levesque, Raposa was a sex worker in the Bedford Street area. Over the coming weeks, Maltias sporadically returned to the police station, offering more information about what he knew. According to him, satanism was on the rise in Fall River, and he knew two women who might have some information about the earlier murder of Levesque. In December 1979, he brought Robin Murphy, 17, and Karen Marsden, 20, to the station. Murphy and Marsden were romantically involved, and Marsden supported them both financially by working as a sex worker along Bedford Street. According to the two women, 26-year-old Carl Drew was responsible for the murder of Levesque. They said that Drew was Levesque's pimp and that he was the leader of a satanic cult based in Fall River. However, with no evidence other than the testimony of two young women with drug problems, police took no action.

Then, on January 26, 1980, hunters stumbled across the partially frozen body of Raposa in a wooded area behind RESC Printing. Her hands were bound with fishing line; she had been sexually assaulted; and, like Levesque, she had been bludgeoned to death with a rock. A few weeks later, Karen Marsden vanished. Shortly before her disappearance, Marsden met frequently with Fall River police, who were investigating the murder of Levesque. She had sobbed that she feared for her life after betraying "the Devil," a.k.a. Carl Drew. She claimed that Drew threatened to inject battery acid into her veins and offer her soul to Satan if she ever went to the police. [1] Carol Fletcher, a young woman who knew them both, said that Drew warned that "in the right time and the right place, he was going to kill Karen."[2] Now, she was missing. It was not until April 18, 1980, that her skull was found in a wooded area known as Family Beach in Westport, Massachusetts. Like the two women before her, her skull bore evidence of blunt force trauma. Nearby, police discovered a bloodstained rock, as well as clothing and a clump of hair belonging to Marsden.

Due to the *modus operandi* and victim profile being strikingly similar in each case, Fall River police began treating the murders as the work of an opportunistic serial killer preying on women with high-risk lifestyles. They also focused on the possibility that stories of a so-called "cult of devil worshippers" could in fact be true.[3] Other sex workers operating on the dimly lit streets of Fall River came forward to tell police that such a cult existed and that several of them had attended "devil-worshipping" rituals in Freetown State Forest and in a Fall River housing project.[4] The women said that they were coming forward because they were afraid they would end up brutally murdered like Karen Marsden. They claimed that Levesque, Raposa, and Marsden were killed because the cult leaders considered them "weak links" who might expose the cult's nefarious activities. Initially, Capt. Ronald Andrade of the Fall River police department was skeptical: "A lot of these people we talked to are heavy drug users and we're wondering whether this cult exists in their minds or is a real thing," he said.[5] But in mid-April 1980, he publicly announced that they had reason to believe that a satanic cult did exist in Fall River and that this cult was likely to blame for the murders. Long before the murders, local legend had warned of a satanic cult in the dense 5,500 acres (2,226 hectares) of Freetown State Forest. At various times, makeshift altars, wooden crosses, mutilated animals, disfigured dolls, and pentagrams had been found by passersby.

By now, police had a list of suspects under investigation. The first to be interviewed was Andy Maltias. He denied any involvement in the murder of Barbara Raposa before telling police that he had "dreams and visions" about her murder. In these visions, Maltias said he was escorted to Raposa's body "by two angels" and that he witnessed the killing. During the vision, Maltias said he was floating above the murder scene and that he saw "a man beating on a woman." He described the man as "fairly tall with long hair."[6] Maltias seemed to have information about the slaying that wasn't public knowledge, even down to its exact location. He was duly arrested and charged with Raposa's murder. Shortly afterward, Robin Murphy was picked up by Fall River police after making incriminating statements about the string of murders. When Murphy was apprehended, she confessed that she had been present at all three killings. She said that the murders of Marsden and Levesque were part of a satanic ritual conducted by Carl Drew, who was their pimp. Murphy also claimed that Maltias killed Raposa because she was dating another man and he had become so jealous that, in a fit of rage, he bludgeoned her to death. Despite the fact that all three murders were strikingly similar, Murphy claimed that there was no connection between the Raposa case and the other two.

Following her confessions, Murphy was allowed to plead guilty to second-degree murder in exchange for turning state's evidence. She was sentenced to life with the possibility of parole.

Murphy took to the stand during Maltias' trial and told the court that Maltias had picked her and Raposa up in his car on November 7, 1989, and that she and Raposa had gotten into a physical fight after smoking a joint in the backseat. Maltias got out of the car and pulled Raposa off her. Around midnight, Maltias took two brown paper bags out of the trunk of the car and walked into the wooded area with Raposa. Murphy said she sat in the car while Maltias raped Raposa in the woods before he killed her with a rock. When asked why she hadn't come forward with this information earlier, Murphy said she was afraid and had only built up the courage to confess from the safety of her jail cell. She also claimed that Maltias had been molesting her and providing her with drugs since she was 11 years old.

On trial for first-degree murder, Maltias claimed that he was at home with his mother on the day of Raposa's murder. His mother corroborated her son's alibi.[7] Nevertheless, on January 30, 1981, Maltias was found guilty of murder in the first degree and sentenced to life imprisonment.

Next up was the trial of Carl Drew, who by this point the media were referring to as the "leader of a devil-worshipping cult of pimps and prostitutes."[8] Superior Court Judge Francis W. Keating asked the jury not to be swayed, because information about the alleged cult was not offered as evidence. Murphy testified that Levesque was killed because she wanted to work the streets on her own without Drew as a pimp. Drew forced Levesque into his car and shouted that she "couldn't' afford to work the streets alone." They drove to Diman Regional Vocational Technical High School, and Murphy said that she remained in the car while Drew dragged Levesque to the bleachers and killed her. Despite evidence that the murder was exceptionally brutal, Murphy claimed that she didn't hear Levesque make a sound and that Drew came back to the car without any blood on his clothes.

According to Murphy, she, Drew, and two others drove Karen Marsden to Family Beach in Westport on February 8, 1980. She said that she dragged Marsden from the car to the woods by her hair. Drew allegedly ordered Marsden to give Murphy a diamond ring she was wearing. She refused, and Drew cut off her finger to get it off.[9] Murphy told the court that Drew then ordered her to slit Marsden's throat after they both took turns hitting her with rocks, breaking her neck. Before Marsden died, Drew allegedly told her, "God can't help you now." She said Drew then began to speak in tongues before dipping his thumb in Marsden's blood and drawing an "X" on Murphy's forehead, telling her she was now a member of their satanic cult. After the slaying, Murphy claimed Drew pulled Marsden's head off with his bare hands and kicked it into the foliage, but not before the group performed sex acts with it. She also told the court that during the murders, she experienced "out of body sensations."[10] and "would not have killed Karen if I hadn't been possessed." Murphy said that she had been present during a number of séances led by Drew in Freetown State Forest and that Levesque and Marsden were killed as "an offering of a soul to Satan."

Carol Fletcher also testified during Drew's trial. She said that she was present at the killing of Marsden but had not actively participated in it. Like Murphy, Fletcher was granted immunity in exchange for information about the murder. However, while Murphy was in prison, after pleading guilty, she wrote a letter to a friend in which she complained that some of the information given by Fletcher contradicted her own testimony. "She's saying everything," she wrote. "She's trying to get Carl and me life in prison."

Lea Johnson, another witness at the trial, described Drew as a "nice guy" but claimed he vividly described the murder of Karen Marsden to her. "He wanted her to feel pain."[11]

Although there was no direct evidence connecting him to the killing, Drew was convicted of Karen Marsden's murder and sentenced to life in prison without the possibility of parole. Drew has always proclaimed his innocence: "Robin Murphy is, and always will be, a danger to society," he has said.[12] According to Drew,

Murphy committed all the murders and then blamed them on other people when she knew the police were closing in.

Later, Murphy recanted her damning testimony against Drew, denying that she had even been present during Marsden's murder. In an unsuccessful bid for a new trial, she claimed she had lied because she was under pressure from prosecutors. "I believed he belonged in jail, but also knew justice was not taking place. So I made the story up," she stated.[13] In 2004, Murphy was granted parole and remained free for just over six years. In 2011, she was stopped by a state trooper in Revere and it was discovered the woman she was driving with had a felony record and was in possession of heroin. Murphy was sent back to prison for violating her parole, which stated she wasn't allowed to have contact with convicted criminals. She applied for parole once again in 2012 but was denied, despite claiming she didn't know the woman and was simply giving her a lift. In March 2012, she went before the parole board again and confessed the woman had been her lover but that she didn't know she had heroin in her possession. "Quite frankly, we can't grant you parole if you don't tell us the truth," said Board Chair Paul Treseler.[14] The parole board lambasted Murphy for her continual lies: "You are almost four decades into lie after lie after lie," said another board member. Once again, she was denied parole.

The fourth person who was allegedly present during the murder of Karen Marsden was Carl Davis. While he was incarcerated, he wrote a statement admitting that this was so, adding, "I don't know why Carl Drew's name was mentioned, he wasn't there." The case against Davis fell apart, and he never stood trial for his alleged role in the murder.

In 2004, Carol Fletcher recanted her testimony that implicated Carl Drew in the murder of Karen Marsden. She said she was threatened by police into making false statements and that Robin Murphy had killed Marsden on the roof of the former Harbor Terrace apartments in Fall River.

The case of Doreen Levesque never went to trial. Nobody was ever charged with or convicted of her murder.

Decades have passed since the Fall River Cult Murders, and the gruesome case still remains controversial. Did it give some legitimacy to the fear of satanic cults, or was the cult the product of a drug-addicted teenager's warped imagination? Due to the social preoccupations of the time, it is possible that the cult aspect of the case was sensationalized by the police and the media. From prison, Carl Drew still maintains his innocence and argues that it was actually Murphy who was the ringleader of the satanic cult and who perpetrated the murders on her own.

While investigating the murders undercover, Detective Paul Carey of the Fall River Major Crimes Division attended a satanic ritual in a Fall River apartment. He said that both Carl Drew and Robin Murphy were in attendance. "There were strange chants and a 'Hail Satan' announcement indicating that Satan had entered the room," he told APB News. He believes that Drew is innocent of the slayings and that it was actually Murphy who committed the murders.

Whatever the truth may be, the fact remains that three women were brutally murdered under strikingly similar circumstances, presumably by the same person or persons. Even today, the Fall River Cult murders continue to cast a macabre shadow over the woodlands of Massachusetts.

---

[1] *Mortal Remains: A True Story of Ritual Murder* by Henry Scammell
[2] *Commonwealth vs. Carl H. Drew*

[3] *The Orlando Sentinel*, April 19, 1980—"Police Probing Cult in Slaying of Women"

[4] *The Boston Globe*, May 10, 1980—"3 Indicted in Slaying; Cult Link Seen"

[5] *The Boston Globe*, April 19, 1980—"Satan Cult Probed in 2 Deaths"

[6] *The Boston Globe*, January 26, 1981—"Witness Tells of Defendant's 'Dream Vision'"

[7] *Commonwealth* v. *Maltias*

[8] *Muncie Evening Press*, March 14, 1981—"Cult Devil Guilty of Killing"

[9] *South Coast Today*, March 10, 1981—"Looking Back: Murder in Satan's Name"

[10] *The Springfield News-Leader*, March 11, 1981—"Cultist Describes Murder"

[11] *The Herald News*, November 3, 2017—"Robin Murphy Denied Parole"

[12] *The Daily Herald*, March 11, 1981—"Witness Recounts Killing Revealed by 'Nice Guy'"

[13] *The Herald News*, March 7, 2012—"Convicted Fall River Cult Murderer Up for Parole"

[14] *The Herald News*, March 24, 2004—"Cult Killer Robin Murphy Says She Made Up the Story"

The Ant Hill Kids

Sequestered in the Canadian wilderness, the community known as the Ant Hill Kids seemed just a group of naive, self-sufficient, free-thinking folks. However, life inside the commune was very different. Torture, abuse, mutilation, and even murder were accepted without question.

"He was standing, looking like he was in a trance.
I was helpless—long enough for him to decide
that the arm had to come off."

Gabrielle Lavallée, cult member

The leader of the Ant Hill Kids cult, Roch Thériault, was a self-styled prophet who ordered his followers to call him Moses. His appalling brutality, which led him to be named one of Canada's most notorious criminals, was not finally revealed until one of his many wives escaped the commune. Barely clinging to life, Gabrielle Lavallée reached civilization with her right arm missing and eight of her teeth ripped from her jaw.

Thériault was born on May 16, 1947, in Saguenay Valley, Quebec Province, to Hyacinthe and Pierrette Thériault. His family were part of a fundamentalist Catholic movement known as the Pilgrims of St. Michael, or the "white berets," after the distinctive hats they wear during meetings and while distributing their literature. He was the second of seven children and the oldest boy. He would later claim his father was abusive toward him. However, the elder Thériault later denied this. Thériault was said to be a bright, intelligent child but dropped out of school—like the rest of his siblings—when he was just 13 years old. Shortly thereafter, he began obsessing over the apocalypse and the Old Testament. Thériault was raised a Catholic but converted to the Seventh-day Adventist Church, adopting their way of life and belief system and relinquishing alcohol, tobacco, and processed foods. Thériault earned money by distributing Seventh-day Adventist material door-to-door and also ran antismoking seminars. However, his time with his local Adventist group was brief: he was barred after attempting to gain leadership. Nevertheless, he managed to attract a group of vulnerable spiritual searchers eager to follow him on his journey. By the mid-1970s, Thériault was convinced that he had been chosen by God to save the world from evil and the imminent apocalypse. With his long beard and piercing blue eyes, Thériault— a powerful orator—proclaimed himself a prophet and bade others join his religious movement. [1]

Thériault's professed goal was to establish a commune of like-minded followers, where people could listen to his teachings and live as equals. He convinced his acolytes that he was God's representative on Earth and that the world was corrupt. This corruption extended to his adherents' own families, whom they were forced to abandon. In 1978, Thériault predicted that the world would end "in a shower of boulderlike hailstones" in February the following year. To prepare for this momentous event, Thériault and his small band of disciples—four men, nine women, and four children— moved to the "Eternal Mountain" near the village of St. Jogues in the Gaspésie region of Quebec province. Here, "The Holy Moses Mountain Family," as they now called themselves, collected around $2,000 a month in family allowances and welfare and built a commune of tents and log cabins. When the apocalypse did not materialize, Thériault claimed that this was because of differences between the Israelite calendar and the Roman Catholic calendar.

By this point, life within the commune had begun to take bizarre and sinister turns. In a bid to increase his following, Thériault "married" every female in the commune and impregnated them, fathering 20 children by nine different women. An operation he had undergone for stomach ulcers had led to him becoming fascinated by medicine and, while drunk, he believed he could perform medical procedures on commune members. In 1981, he attempted to "operate" on two-year-old Samuel Giguère. The boy had been having difficulty passing urine when Thériault grabbed a pair of scissors and sliced Giguère's penis. When Giguère wouldn't stop crying in the aftermath, he was severely beaten by cult member Guy Veer. Instead of rushing the boy to hospital, cult members attempted to save his life themselves. When this failed and he died from his injuries, they tried to conceal the cause of death by setting the body on fire. Afterward, Thériault castrated Veer as punishment and ordered his followers to say that Veer had been trampled by a horse. The truth finally came out, however, and Quebec police raided the commune and discovered the child's body. Thériault, Veer, Gabrielle Lavallée, and five others were arrested and charged with criminal negligence causing bodily harm. Veer was found not guilty by reason of insanity, while Thériault was sentenced to almost two years in prison, and Lavallée was sentenced to nine months.

Following his release, Thériault rejoined his followers despite the fact that his parole order barred him from associating with fellow cult members. In 1984, he established a 200-acre (81-hectare) commune near Burnt River, Ontario, approximately 37 miles (60 km) northwest of the city of Peterborough. Burnt River was a quaint hamlet with a general store, two small churches, and a post office. Here, Thériault ruled over his concubines, along with 26 children (most of which were his own), and other followers that had remained loyal despite his legal troubles. In a 1984 interview with the *Fenelon Falls Gazette*, Thériault stated that he simply wanted to "live freely and naturally away from the constraints and controls of the system." The community consisted of log cabins, one of which was used for making maple syrup and preserves, one for baking bread, and one for smoking fish, which cult members caught in the nearby river and sold locally. Thériault compared his hard-working followers to ants working on an ant hill, and thus arrived at the name the Ant Hill Kids. The women of the cult used to go door-to-door selling their produce; they also took menial jobs, such as cleaning, while the men did odd jobs. "They were different, unique . . . living off the land that way," recalled Marshall Dudman, a local man.[2] During the Ant Hill Kids' first winter in Burnt River, kindly neighbors helped the cult by giving them vegetables and fruit.

However, rumors began to emerge in the hamlet concerning the cult's former activities and convictions. By this point, Thériault was drinking heavily and his behavior was becoming increasingly violent. He exerted control over the cult in increasingly cruel ways, and his followers were too weak—both physically and mentally—to break free. He forbade them from speaking to one another without his permission and, for his entertainment, conducted gladiatorial tournaments, forcing them to attack one another inside a dirt ring. Delusional and paranoid, Thériault convinced himself that some of his followers were spying on him and planning to escape. He punished anyone he suspected of defecting by hitting them with a belt. He later employed a hammer and the flat side of an axe.[3] If he thought that a follower was even thinking about leaving, he would suspend them from the ceiling and pluck out their body hairs one by one before defecating on them. As his power over the commune grew, Thériault forced his followers to prove their loyalty to him by breaking their own legs with sledgehammers. He ordered them to sit on lit stoves, shoot each other in the shoulder, smear feces on one another, and cut off each other's toes. Sexual abuse was rife; followers were also made to eat their own feces. Thériault told the commune's children that anybody who came to the commune from the outside world was sent by the devil to harm them. To the children, eating, washing, and even talking were a privilege. Much like the women of the commune, the children were systematically sexually abused and would be stripped naked and whipped to "purify" them. One evening, in the middle of a blizzard, commune member Gabrielle Lavallée placed her newborn baby, Eleazar, outside and he succumbed to the cold. According to Lavallée, she was only trying to protect her child from Thériault's violent outbursts. The death resulted in social workers and police investigating the cult for abuse. In 1987, officers from Ontario's Children's Aid Society removed 14 children from the commune and placed them in foster homes. The regime of abuse was stopped, but the commune continued; Thériault's followers now comprised two men and eight women.

Thériault's frequent rages intensified when he was drunk and, following the removal of the children, his drinking increased, and with it his obsession with medical science. On one occasion, he placed a rubber band around the testicles of one follower. After eight hours, the man's scrotum had swollen and eventually became infected. Thériault plied the man with alcohol, removed the testicle, and cauterized the wound with a piece of a hot iron. On September 29, 1988, after a day of drinking and picking petty arguments with his followers, Thériault dressed up as the "King of Israelites."[4] Thinking back to earlier that morning, when 32-year-old Solange Boilard had complained of stomach problems, Thériault forced her onto the kitchen table and stripped her naked.

With just a cloth stuffed in her mouth to muffle her screams, Thériault punched Boilard in the stomach, jammed a plastic tube up her rectum and performed an enema with molasses and olive oil. He then made an incision on the right side of her abdomen, pulled out a section of her intestine with his bare hands, ripped a piece of the intestine out, and pushed the rest back into her abdomen. With this so-called operation completed, Thériault ordered Gabrielle Lavallée to stitch the wound while another member blew into a tube he had shoved down Boilard's throat. Boilard died in agony the following day. Claiming he had the power of resurrection, Thériault ordered his followers to remove Boilard's uterus and saw off a portion of her skull so that he could ejaculate into her brain and bring her back to life. When Boilard didn't revive, Thériault ordered his followers to bury her body in the commune grounds. Before they did so, he removed one of her ribs, which he kept in a leather case around his neck. To show his gratitude for their assistance, he gave each cult member a piece of her rib as a "keepsake."[5]

In November 1988, Gabrielle Lavallée complained of a toothache, and Thériault responded by ripping out several of her teeth with a pair of pliers. Later that same night, he chased Lavallée around the commune with a knife and, in the ensuing struggle, cut the tendon of one of her hands. Lavallée managed to get herself to a hospital, where they placed wires in her right hand to support the tendon. Despite the abuse she had endured, she agreed to return to the commune when Thériault promised to stop drinking. However, Thériault did not keep his promise for long. One night in July 1989, an inebriated Thériault impaled Lavallée's hand on the kitchen table with a knife after she complained that she felt stiffness in one finger. "He was standing, looking like he was in a trance," she said. "I was helpless—long enough for him to decide

The Oneida Community

John Humphrey Noyes, leader of the Oneida Community, as depicted in an 1871 engraving.

The impressive Oneida Community Mansion House in New York State was built in 1862. It is now a historic landmark and museum.

"The Children's Hour" in the Oneida Community Mansion House's upper sitting room.

Constructing animal traps, as well as a variety of household items, enabled the Oneida Community to thrive.

The Manson Family

Charles Manson's appearance changed dramatically from his 1969 arrest to the conclusion of his trial two years later.

Spahn Ranch, the former Western set that was Manson and his followers' main home at the time of their arrest.

Members of the Manson Family.

A December 1969 front page featuring pictures of Susan Atkins and Manson claimed that he called himself "Satan."

LINK 11 MURDERS TO TATE KOOKS

'Satan': Leader of a Weird Cult

House Backs Nixon on Viet, 333-55

Victims of the bloodbath at 10050 Cielo Drive (left to right): Wojciech Frykowski, Sharon Tate, Steven Parent, Jay Sebring, and Abigail Folger.

Charles "Tex" Watson, before and after his arrest for murder.

Family member Linda Kasabian, whose testimony helped to convict Manson and his followers.

Susan Atkins, Patricia Krenwinkel, and Leslie Van Houten laugh after receiving death sentences for their roles in the Tate-LaBianca murders.

While incarcerated, Manson altered an X he had carved in his forehead into a swastika.

Filmmakers were quick to cash in on the Manson Family's murderous exploits.

The Symbionese Liberation Army

A 1974 "publicity shot" for the Symbionese Liberation Army shows "Tania"—new recruit Patty Hearst—posing before the group's insignia.

A security camera picks out Hearst standing guard as SLA members rob a bank in San Francisco.

Heiress Patty Hearst, photographed by police on September 18, 1975. Her trial centered on whether she had been brainwashed into joining the SLA.

The SLA's LA hideout blazes during a shootout with police. Hearst was absent, but several members, including SLA leader Donald DeFreeze, lost their lives.

Synanon

Synanon founder Charles E. Dederich observes an experimental program in which a Synanon member stands on boards and paper cups.

Dederich lectures addicts during a seminar at Synanon House.

The Peoples Temple

Future Peoples Temple leader Jim Jones—an idealistic teenager eager to help the poor.

The Rev. Jim Jones' public image exuded power and success.

Peoples Temple thrived in San Francisco during the 1970s and was praised for its work in the community.

Jones, his wife Marceline (on his left) and their extended family in California, before leaving for Jonestown, Guyana.

THIS WAY TO JONESTOWN

Bodies litter the airstrip at Port Kaituma, where US Congressman Leo Ryan (left) and several others were gunned down by a Peoples Temple hit squad.

Jones' wooden makeshift "throne," surrounded by corpses.

An aerial photograph reveals the extent of the carnage wrought in Jonestown.

An iron vessel that held a fruit-flavored drink spiked with cyanide and Valium.

Jones' corpse, stretched on planks following an autopsy, lies alongside those of his followers.

The Fall River Cult

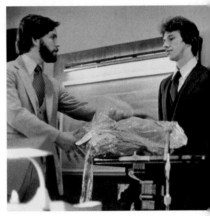

Prosecutor David Draxler questions sex worker Lea Johnson at Carl Drew's trial.

Carl Drew, alleged pimp and leader of a satanist cult in Fall River, Massachusetts, enters the courtroom.

Drew is shown bloodstained clothing belonging to Karen Marsden, whom he is accused of brutally murdering.

The Ant Hill Kids

A sketch of Roch Thériault, leader of the Ant Hill Kids, found pinned to the wall of his abandoned log cabin.

Yahweh ben Yahweh is led in handcuffs to face charges of racketeering and conspiracy to murder.

Self-proclaimed Son of God Yahweh beh Yahweh, whose smiling public demeanor belied violent, racist beliefs.

Clad in white, followers of Yahweh ben Yahweh attend his trial hearing in New Orleans.

The derelict shell of Yahweh ben Yahweh's church in Miami, Florida. The cult has renounced racism and is now dispersed throughout the US.

that the arm had to come off."[6] Thériault then used a carpet knife and meat cleaver to hack off Lavallée's arm. She lay on the floor, writhing in agony, until the following morning, when the stump was stitched up by cult member Chantal Labrie under Thériault's watchful gaze. Days later, he decided that the stitches should be removed and Lavallée's stump had to be cauterized using a piece of drive shaft heated with a blow torch. On August 16, Lavallée finally escaped the cult for good, fleeing into the wilderness before hitchhiking to a hospital just north of Toronto. "It's a miracle that I survived such barbaric aggression," she recalled.

The terrifying truth of what was happening at Burnt River was finally laid bare by Lavallée. Her injuries prompted police to raid the commune on August 23, 1989, but when they arrived, they found that Thériault and three of his followers—Jacques Giguère, Chantal Labrie, and Nicole Ruel—had fled. The surrounding area was densely wooded, rugged, and largely inaccessible to vehicles. The extensive search that ensued was assisted by helicopters and sniffer dogs. Despite a police stakeout, Thériault escaped in a 1980 Dodge van. He and his followers remained on the run for 51 days before finally being apprehended on October 6.

Thériault subsequently pleaded guilty to three counts of aggravated assault and one count of unlawfully causing bodily harm and received a 12-year sentence. Shortly afterward, a cult member helped the authorities discover the body of Solange Boilard. In mid-January 1990, Thériault pleaded guilty to second-degree murder and received a life sentence without the possibility of parole until 2000. All of the cult's children were sent to foster homes.

Three of Thériault's followers—Francine Laflamme, 36, Chantal Labrie, 34, and Nicole Ruel—stuck by him after his incarceration. To remain close to their leader, they moved to a cabin near the prison. During his incarceration, Thériault was granted conjugal visits and went on to have three more children.

According to Thériault's lawyer, Renée Millette, Thériault was often attacked by other convicts while in prison in Dorchester Penitentiary. "The assaults had nothing to do with how he acted while incarcerated. It was because of his past."[7] During a parole hearing, Thériault said he did not want to be released because he feared for his safety.

In February 2011, Thériault was stabbed in the neck by his cellmate, Matthew Gerrard MacDonald, who was serving time for second-degree murder. Moments later, MacDonald walked up to a prison guard, threw down the bloody knife, and said, "That piece of shit is down on the range."[8] The self-proclaimed messiah died from his injuries 30 minutes later, before an ambulance could arrive.

———————————

[1] *Maclean's*, February 8, 1993—"The Ant Hill Kids"
[2] *The Gazette*, September 1, 1989—"Cult Leader's Departure Is Relief to Ontario Town"
[3] *Savage Messiah* by Paul Kaihla and Ross Laver
[4] *Maclean's*, February 8, 1993—"The Ant Hill Kids"
[5] *The Toronto Star*, January 19, 1993—"Cult Leader Gets Life for Killing Disciple"
[6] *The Gazette*, October 12, 1989—"Drunken Cult Leader Thought He Was MD 1—Armed Victim Says"
[7] *The Gazette*, March 1, 2011—"Cult Leader Was 'Victim of His Past'"
[8] *The Gazette*, March 5, 2012—"Life Sentence for Murder of Cult Leader Roch Thériault"

The Nation of Yahweh

The black supremacist leader of this Black Hebrew cult, Yahweh ben Yahweh, led his followers down a dark path of murder and arson. To prove their loyalty, members were required to murder a so-called "white devil."

———————————

"I am here to save you...

I am here to take you out of hell."

Yahweh ben Yahweh

———————————

Outside the state of Florida, the general public knew little about black civil rights group the Nation of Yahweh. It was believed, with some truth, that the group provided food and housing for some of the most deprived people in Florida and also granted children a free education in their own Yahweh school. Then Aston Green, a breakaway follower, was beheaded with a machete in Miami on November 12, 1981. Over the next five years, the cult would become infamous following a series of random killings and mutilations. Its leader referred to himself as the Black Messiah, but to federal prosecutors, Yahweh ben Yahweh was one of the most notorious criminals in Florida's history, as well as the leader of one of the most brutal cults in American criminal history.

Yahweh ben Yahweh was born Hulon Mitchell Jr. in Kingfisher, Oklahoma, on October 27, 1935. The eldest son of strict Pentecostal parents, Mitchell said that when he was just 3 years old, he came to believe that he was the Son of God. In 1960, he graduated from Phillips University in Enid with a psychology degree. Mitchell studied a number of different religions and took part in early civil rights sit-ins. However, he soon became disillusioned, referring to the leading civil rights campaigner Martin Luther King Jr. as a "dead-dog preacher."[1]

Moving to Atlanta in the mid-1960s, Mitchell joined Nation of Islam, a political and religious movement for the advancement of African Americans. He changed his name to Hulon X and also received a master's degree in economics from Atlanta University. In the late 1960s, however, he left the Nation of Islam.[2] It has been suggested that he left the organization under a cloud, amid accusations of embezzlement and even pedophilia; however, these claims remain unsubstantiated.

Mitchell relocated to Miami in the late 1970s, at a time when the city was simmering with racial tensions. The following year, these dramatically intensified when four white police officers were acquitted of beating African American Arthur McDuffie to death on December 21, 1979, an incident that fueled the infamous May 1980 Miami race riots.

In Miami, Mitchell gathered a number of adherents from the African American community and established the Nation of Yahweh, drawing crowds with his explosive speeches on civil rights and racism in the United States. By this point, Mitchell had renamed himself Yahweh ben Yahweh ("God son of God").

From the late 1970s, the Nation of Yahweh rose to prominence, and the numbers of Yahweh ben Yahweh's white-robed and white-suited followers substantially grew. The Nation of Yahweh combined notions of black supremacy with Old Testament messianism. Yahweh preached a doctrine of racial pride and self-reliance. His central tenet was that he was God, the historical Jesus Christ, and also the Second Coming of Christ. To his followers, Yahweh was the "Grand Master of All the God of the Universe, the Grand Potentate, the Everlasting Father, and the persecuted Messiah."[3]

With donated funds, the cult created a multimillion-dollar business empire. They established temples across the country and owned a plethora of apartments, supermarkets, retail stores, hotels, and fleets of white Greyhound buses and luxury cars. Yahweh once estimated that the Nation of Yahweh had holdings of around $100 million. Their "Temple of Love" headquarters sprawled for half a block at 2766 NW and 62nd St., Miami. Here, Yahweh conducted services and children attended the Yahweh school. Members worked at one of the cult's many enterprises and, in turn, contributed their earnings to the cult. The Nation of Yahweh earned acclaim for its various community revitalization projects, purchasing and renovating housing in some of Miami's poorest African American neighborhoods. The cult's presence in these once-dilapidated areas removed "hot spots" for prostitution and drug dealing. "They solved a big headache for us," said Lt. Allan Schlefstein, head of Miami's street crimes unit.

The Nation of Yahweh's ideology drew on ideas promulgated by the Nation of Islam's leader Elijah Muhammad, which in turn were derived from the Black Hebrew Israelite belief system that had existed in the US since the 1800s. Black Hebrew Israelites believe that Sub-Saharan Africans are the true descendants of the ancient Israelites and therefore God's chosen people. A Nation of Yahweh elder, Job Israel, told the *Intelligence Report* in 2007, "God created the white man to punish us for being disobedient to God. The original devil was black. But when Cain killed Abel, God cursed him to be white. Yahweh [God] gave him [the white man] a hedge of protection and gave him 6,000 years to rule . . . This is the year 6007. The devil's rulership is up."

This idea of the 6,000-year rule by "white devils" derived from Nation of Islam leader Elijah Muhammad's writings in *The Supreme*

Wisdom Message, originally published in 1957, and *Message to the Blackman in America,* originally published in 1965. Both Elijah Muhammad and Yahweh ben Yahweh claimed that African Americans were superior to all black people. Yahweh championed God and the biblical prophets as black and held the belief that he was the Messiah sent to vanquish the "white devils" and lead black people back to the Promised Land. Like many cult leaders before and after him, Yahweh targeted the community's most disillusioned citizens, telling them that they were the chosen ones and that he would save them from oppression. "I am here to save you," he told his disciples. "I am here to take you out of hell."[4] Yahweh's confidence and wealth spoke volumes to the disenfranchised black communities of southern Florida. According to Miami Urban League head T. Willard Fair, the Nation of Yahweh appealed mostly to black people under the age of 35 who were not affiliated with any church. They ranged from those living in middle-class neighborhoods to those living in some of the most impoverished areas in the city.[4]

While the Nation of Yahweh was thriving, it had a sinister side that revealed itself in Yahweh's apocalyptic preaching against the "white devils" of America. His message was laced with racial hatred and anti-Semitism. Yahweh believed that all white people should be held responsible for centuries of black oppression. In the early 1980s, the Nation of Yahweh was infiltrated by Eugene McCloud, an African American Broward County sheriff's detective. During prayer meetings, McCloud heard Yahweh advocating the murder of white people and referring to other black ministers as "dumb dogs that were misleading black folks about their true identity." Yahweh had many fanatical devotees and, owing to this devotion, was able to demand unfaltering loyalty. One defector, Lloyd Clark, later said that Yahweh would ask followers how many of them would kill a white person if he asked them to, bidding them to raise their hands. Yahweh established a secret suborder of the cult known as "the brotherhood" or the "death angels." To be granted access to this inner circle, a member had to randomly kill a white person and bring physical proof to Yahweh, typically a body part. The murders were intended to evoke fear and intimidation in both followers and outsiders.

Discipline within the Nation of Yahweh was brutal. Yahweh ruled by fear: A group of machete-wielding bodyguards enforced control. He demanded complete obedience from followers, deciding what they wore, what they ate, and who they were romantically involved with. He demanded sexual favors from female disciples while ordering their husbands to be celibate.

In a typically outlandish show of authority, Yahweh personally circumcised his male followers.[5] He also advocated suicide over repression, writing in his book *You Are Not a Nigger! Our True History. The World's Best Kept Secret*, "It is better for us to just go and commit suicide than to allow the enemy to come in our homes and drag us down." If a devotee failed to meet their sales quota or broke rules, they were swiftly punished. Members were forced to kneel on a concrete floor for hours; women would be stripped naked and hit with sticks; disobedient children's fingers would be squashed with butter knives.

In 1981, matters took an even more sinister turn after a cult defector named Aston Green was found in west Dade County. He had been brutally beaten with a tire iron and decapitated with a machete.[6] Yahweh had ordered the biblical sanction for those who committed blasphemy: death by decapitation. Greens' roommates, Carlton Carey and Mildred Banks, later told police that the killer was most likely a member of the Nation of Yahweh. Shortly thereafter, they were ambushed outside as they arrived home. Carey was shot dead and Banks was shot and slashed across the neck with a machete. Miraculously, she survived; however, she refused to identify her assailants, her fear only confirming belief in Yahweh ben Yahweh's omnipotence. Investigators later claimed that the killers had intended to behead the couple if Banks hadn't escaped. The Nation of Yahweh was suspected, but investigators could not find enough evidence to link them to the murders and attempted murder.

Two years later, on September 17, 1983, Leonard Dupree, a former US karate champion and cult member accused of being a dissident, was beaten to death with a stick and tire iron in the cult's temple. Yahweh ben Yahweh reportedly forced everybody present to join in the brutal beating so that if anyone talked, they would be implicating themselves.

Three years later, the outside world became the focus of Yahweh's violent program as he finally put his squad of "death angels" to use. In April 1986, Glendell Fowler, a hospital technician, and Kurt Doerr, a waiter, were stabbed to death in their Coconut Grove apartment. Determined to crush any opposition within the black community, the Nation of Yahweh firebombed six homes in a black neighborhood in Delray Beach in May 1986. Two days earlier, youths from the area had had an altercation with Nation of Yahweh members. A later description of the attack, cited in a 1996 federal court ruling upholding Yahweh ben Yahweh's conviction, said that "Yahweh ordered the arsonists to stand in front of the residences and use their swords and machetes to murder anyone who tried to exit the burning houses."[7] At the time, the Nation of Yahweh denied any involvement and gave two families burned out of their homes $5,500 each.

The mutilated bodies of random white people began appearing on the streets of Miami, sometimes as eye-for-an-eye reprisals for the killing of a black man in Miami or elsewhere. Homeless people and drifters were particularly easy targets. Some were attacked while sleeping on the streets or drunk. Often their ears, or parts of their ears, were cut off as proof of a "confirmed kill." A homeless man named Clair Walters was stabbed to death on May 22, 1986, while squatting in an abandoned hotel on Biscayne Boulevard. His throat had been slashed and his left ear amputated. Two months later, another homeless man, James Lee Myers, was stabbed to death on the same street. His ear had been slashed but not severed. In September, another drifter, Lyle Austin Bellinger, was stabbed to death near Biscayne Boulevard. The same day, Raymond Kelley, a motor-pool mechanic, was stabbed to death in South Miami. Both of his ears were hacked off. Two weeks later, Cecil Branch, a garbage man, was stabbed to death in his Coconut Grove home. The top of his right ear had been cut off and he was found bound and gagged by his landlord. On October 1, Harry Byers, a 68-year-old homeless man, was stabbed to death on a park bench at Legion Park on Biscayne Boulevard. His left ear had been severed. The following week, Reinaldo Echevarria was stabbed to death on 103rd Street and 32nd Avenue in Miami.

Shortly thereafter, the Nation of Yahweh illegally evicted tenants from an apartment block in Opa-locka, Florida that the cult had recently acquired. Two days later, Anthony Brown and Rudolph Broussard, who had opposed the cult's takeover of the complex, were found shot dead.

The veil of secrecy finally began to slip with the arrest of group member Robert Rozier, who was charged with the murders of Anthony Brown, Rudolph Broussard, Glendell Fowler, and Kurt

Doerr. In the wake of his arrest, the Nation of Yahweh excommunicated the former professional football player and launched a public relations campaign, highlighting the charitable work it had achieved over the past number of years. While the strategy worked for a while, many Nation of Yahweh members turned against Yahweh for the excommunication of Rozier. Soon, investigators began to build a case against Yahweh. Rozier received a mitigated sentence of 22 years in exchange for giving evidence against Yahweh. Rozier accused the Nation of Yahweh of performing ritual slayings ordered by its leader. More accusations from other ex-cult members followed. Lloyd Clark and Wilbert Rolle accused the cult of murder, extortion, and child abuse. Investigators said that children in the cult were beaten with switches, forced to beg on the street, and threatened with scissors.[8] Three women and six men were charged with assault and endangering the welfare of a child. Clark said that Yahweh sexually abused the children in the cult: "He was having some of the girls there that were 12 years old." The Dade state attorney's office lacked the investigative resources available to the federal government. Yahweh denied child abuse in his cult, and witnesses were too afraid to talk, so the allegations were quietly forgotten.[9]

The cult, and Yahweh ben Yahweh himself, were still riding high in 1990, with Miami Mayor Xavier Suarez even declaring October 7 "Yahweh ben Yahweh Day." However, the following month, suspicions surrounding Yahweh and his cult escalated into a federal racketeering indictment. Yahweh and 14 members were accused of ordering 14 murders; two attempted murders; the firebombing of six homes in Delray Beach; and making sex slaves out of female followers, including minors.[10]

Following the arrests, many Floridians found it difficult to accept that somebody who had brought so much economic dynamism to their community could be involved in such barbaric crimes. During Yahweh ben Yahweh's trial, which commenced on January 2, 1992, and ended on May 28, gruesome crime scene and autopsy photographs were shown to jurors. The court was further shocked by the matter-of-fact testimony of cult members such as Ricardo Woodside, who recalled that during the beheading of Aston Green, he heard someone say, "Damn, this blade is dull."[11]

Despite the fact that federal and state investigators spent millions of dollars investigating the murders, Yahweh was acquitted owing to doubts about Rozier's testimony, especially the fact that he had received a reduced sentence for it. Instead, Yahweh and 10 others were charged with conspiracy and racketeering and five others were charged with conspiracy. Found guilty, Yahweh ben Yahweh was sentenced to 18 years in prison.

In January 1996, the 11th US Circuit Court of Appeals in Atlanta ruled that the Nation of Yahweh had committed "ruthless crimes" and expressed doubts about Yahweh's acquittal for murder. "Our review of the record convinces us that the evidence presented at trial was more than sufficient to support Yahweh's conviction. While he did not commit the acts personally, he ordered his followers to commit numerous acts of murder, secure in the knowledge that his orders would be carried out." [12]

While he was incarcerated, most of the Nation of Yahweh's business holdings fell into foreclosure. Many of Yahweh's followers renounced him in the wake of the trial. However, some stayed loyal to their Messiah, convinced that Yahweh had had no part in the murders and that Robert Rozier was an alienated group member who had committed the murders alone.

Yahweh Ben Yahweh was paroled in 2001, but died of cancer six years later. He proclaimed himself to be the savior of African Americans, but behind a cloak of respectability, he was a cruel cult leader who built an empire on a foundation of intimidation and murder. His obsession with personal power led to violent acts that overshadowed his early good works. Yahweh ben Yahweh died in 2007 aged 71, but the ideas he promulgated still find favor among elements in black communities in the US, who harbor justifiable resentments against the numerous injustices meted out by a predominantly white establishment. The Nation of Yahweh is still active today.

---

[1] *The Gazette*, May 11, 2007—"Convicted Leader of Black Sect"

[2] Southern Poverty Law Center, September 22, 2007—"Nation of Yahweh Mourns Loss of Leader"

[3] Southern Poverty Law Center, September 22, 2006—"Miami-Based Nation of Yahweh Leader Appeals Parole"

[4] *Los Angeles Times*, December 21, 1994—"The Demonic Leadership of a Self-Proclaimed Preacher"

[5] *South Florida Sun Sentinel*, November 11, 1990—"Yahweh Preached to Followers What They Sought to Hear"

[6] *People*, June 22, 2018—"A Beheading and Circumcisions in the Nation of Yahweh"

[7] *Brother Love: Murder, Money and a Messiah* by Sydney P. Freedberg

[8] *The Miami Herald*, May 9, 2007—"Beguiling Leader, Alleged Killer"

[9] *The Atlanta Constitution*, December 26, 1986—"The Yahwehs' Presence in Atlanta"

[10] *Miami Herald*, November 9, 1990—"State Probes Long-Held Claims of Child Abuse in Yahweh Sect"

[11] *United States of America, Plaintiff* v. *Yahweh Ben Yahweh, et al., Defendants.*

[12] *Miami Herald*, January 6, 1996—"Murder in the Temple of Love"

Rajneeshpuram

The disciples of Bhagwan Shree Rajneesh built a citylike commune for the guru in the Oregon hills. But the Rajneeshees' dreams of peace, love, and hedonism collapsed in shocking, insidious controversies.

———————————

"I would like the whole world
to live so luxuriously that people start
becoming bored with luxury."

Bhagwan Shree Rajneesh

———————————

B hagwan Shree Rajneesh was an Indian spiritual leader whose teachings advocated materialism, meditation, capitalism, and sexual activity. The "Hugh Hefner of the spiritual world" had hoped to create a utopia of peace, love, and hedonism in his commune in the barren landscape of central Oregon but instead became mired in criminality involving immigration fraud, biological terrorism, and assassination plots.[1] In the early 1980s, a number of his power-hungry disciples provoked a storm of angry conflict in Oregon, which ultimately led to the downfall of Rajneesh and his commune, amid arrests and deportations.

The son of a cloth merchant and the eldest of 11 children, Rajneesh was born Chandra Mohan Jain in Kuchwada, India, on December 11, 1931. For the first seven years of his life, he lived with his middle-class grandparents in Kuchwada while his parents lived in the village of Timani, where his father worked. Jain developed a deep attachment to his grandparents and would later refer to them as his "real parents."[2] During these formative years, his grandparents gave him considerable freedom both physically and intellectually. When he misbehaved, they did not punish him. Later, as a philosophy student in Jabalpur University, Jain was said to be gifted but also argumentative and disruptive, frequently challenging his tutors. He rejected his parents' wishes for him to marry and pursued an academic teaching career. Having achieved an MA in philosophy at Sagar University, Jain became a meditation leader at Jabalpur University.[3] It was beneath a solitary tree in Jabalpur that he claimed to have achieved spiritual enlightenment.

Jain soon became a prominent antitheist (one who is opposed to belief in the existence of a god or gods) and started to research ways to expand consciousness, including yoga, meditation, breath control, hypnosis, and even the occult. In 1971, Jain started calling himself Bhagwan Shree Rajneesh, a name of self-declared enlightenment. He traveled throughout India, gave speeches on spirituality, and held meditation camps, garnering much attention for his opposition to socialism. Rajneesh established his first ashram in Pune in 1974. During this time, thousands of Westerners were flocking to India in search of spiritual enlightenment and a sense of belonging. Rajneesh found himself at the hub of a lucrative enterprise, employing a potent combination of Western psychology, hypnotic induction, chanting, and Eastern meditation techniques to induce states of altered consciousness. Encounter groups were held in padded rooms, where participants were encouraged to release suppressed emotions; some screamed, some sang, some danced, and some erupted in violence. The 1981 documentary *Ashram in Poona* by Wolfgang Dobrowolny captures an unnerving encounter in which a woman is almost raped. Later, the same woman claims the man was just "working out his anger."

Rajneesh's followers referred to themselves as "sannyasins" (someone who has renounced the material world for the spiritual world) or "Rajneeshees," and they largely consisted of highly educated young people drawn from all over the world. They wore various shades of orange (a sacred color in Hinduism) and red to symbolize the dawning of a new day, as well as beaded necklaces with a locket containing a photograph of their guru.

Over the next decade, Rajneesh's popularity grew; he claimed to have 500,000 followers across the world. His success ruffled feathers with a number of critics. Frances Fitzgerald wrote in *The New Yorker* magazine in 1986 that Rajneesh claimed that orthodox Indian religions were dead and filled with empty ritual. Rajneesh claimed these religions oppressed believers with fears of damnation and promises of blessings.[4] Rajneesh's controversial practices and doctrine led to opposition not only by religious groups but also by the Janata Party government. Furthermore, the Pune police chief claimed that female sannyasins were involved in an "epidemic" of prostitution to swell the cult's coffers. The group was also accused of using brainwashed women followers as drug mules.

By 1981, tensions in India had reached a breaking point and the group's tax-free status had been revoked. Rajneesh's powerful spokesman and secretary, Ma Anand Sheela, took decisive action and decided to relocate. For the sum of $5.9 million, she purchased the 64,000-acre Big Muddy Ranch, near Antelope in Wasco County, Oregon. In October, the ranch was renamed Rajneeshpuram. Thousands of followers worked tirelessly to turn arid ranchland into a theocratic utopia, planting trees and shrubs so Rajneesh would not have to view the barren landscape.

Rajneeshpuram was soon ready to receive Bhagwan Shree Rajneesh. Announcing himself as "the messiah America has been waiting for," Rajneesh arrived in the US in grand style in one of his many Rolls-Royces.[5] His followers paid between $500 and $1,500 a month for the privilege of living and working near Rajneesh and participating in the communal dream of a new Eden. New recruits paid entrance fees ranging from $5,000 to $150,000, depending on their work skills and personal circumstances. Bemused Antelope residents were told that all the Rajneeshees wanted was to follow their religion, farm their land, and live a quiet life.

Rajneesh drew heavily on the trappings of Eastern religions, but his philosophy was very different. He placed great emphasis on free love, stating that sex was a "meditative first step on the path to super-consciousness—or enlightenment." He encouraged adherents to follow their sexual desires and denounced marriage and procreation, claiming that families were dysfunctional and destructive. He was pro-abortion and supported contraception and male and female sterilization. Some sannyasins who moved to Rajneeshpuram left their children behind with family members. For them, their spiritual journey was more important than their own family.

Rajneesh also scoffed at conventional religions: "There is no god, so how can I consider myself a god? God is the greatest lie invented by Man," he once said. Moreover, Rajneesh didn't expect his followers to live without worldly desires and referred to himself as the "rich man's guru." He had no qualms about acquiring as many material possessions as possible. Rajneesh amassed a collection of wristwatches estimated to be worth the modern equivalent of $11 million, as well as 93 Rolls-Royces and a Learjet.[6] He once said, "I would like the whole world to live so luxuriously that people start becoming bored with luxury."[7] He openly denounced Gandhi, stating that he was "a masochist reactionary who worshipped poverty."[8] Many sannyasins were wealthy and donated large sums of money to the cult. Additionally, the cult made a substantial income from the sale of books and tapes of Rajneesh's teachings. By 1983, his fortune was estimated at $30.8 million.

Initially, Rajneeshpuram seemed little different from other groups that had fled persecution to establish their own utopias. However, a darker side to the cult soon became apparent. The surrounding communities, particularly Antelope—a quaint town of around 40 residents—and The Dalles, the county seat of Wasco County, grew increasingly suspicious of their strange new neighbors, claiming they were confrontational and judgmental. For their part, Rajneeshees characterized their neighbors as religious bigots. As Rajneeshpuram grew, a clash of cultures was inevitable. Disgruntled locals claimed that the commune was violating constitutional guarantees of the separation of church and state. An environmental watchdog group named 1,000 Friends of Oregon argued that Rajneeshpuram was violating the state's strict land-use laws, which cited that only agricultural work could be carried out on the ranch. By this point, Rajneesh had no direct involvement with the daily operations of the commune; he had voluntarily withdrawn into silence and seclusion. Rajneeshpuram now followed a rigid institutional structure of its own and developed a hierarchy with Sheela as its self-appointed president and spokesperson.

Unable to get the ranch incorporated as a city, which would have allowed the Rajneeshees to legally expand their business activities, the group turned its attention to the nearest urban center—Antelope. When the Antelope City Council refused to grant the Rajneeshees a permit to set up a printing press in the town with a workforce of 111—nearly three times the original population—Sheela responded by bringing a lawyer to council meetings and announcing that they needed an incorporated city to carry out their highly lucrative mail-order business "spreading the religious teachings and messages of Bhagwan Shree Raneesh." The council attempted to frustrate the Rajneeshees' business plans by voting to disincorporate the town. However, in May 1982, vastly outnumbering the local residents, the Rajneeshees won control of Antelope. They renamed it the "City of Rajneesh"; established a new city council; named a mayor and municipal judge; and, to the horror of the more strait-laced locals, legalized nudity in the municipal park. They also took control of the curriculum at the only school and created an intimidating police force that patrolled 24 hours a day with assault weapons. This private army patrolled 24 hours a day with assault weapons—Rajneeshpuram had begun to stockpile weapons following a bomb attack on July 29, 1983, on the Hotel Rajneesh in Portland, Oregon, by Stephen Paster, allegedly a member of the Islamic militant group Jamaat al-Fuqra. Visitors' license plates were recorded and photographs were taken of anybody coming or going. Those who opposed the Rajneeshees were sued for crimes such as slander or civil rights violations.

The Rajneeshees transformed Antelope into a thriving community, replete with its own fire and police departments, restaurants, malls, 4,200-foot (1,280-meter) airstrip, unlicensed casino, and the third-largest public transportation system in the US. They even established a university—The Rajneesh International Meditation University—where members could enroll in a number of workshops, some costing thousands of dollars. During its peak, Rajneeshpuram had 6,000 followers living there. Twice a day, Rajneesh himself would parade down Main Street in one of his Rolls-Royces accompanied by trucks of armed guards. Rajneeshees would stop what they were doing and line the road to catch a glimpse of their "enlightened master." To the reserved townsfolk of Antelope, this was a profoundly disturbing sight.

Around this time, Bhagwan Shree Rajneesh addressed rumors that Rajneeshpuram could end in carnage like Jonestown. He laughed at the idea, stating that he taught his followers to live life now, not to wait for heaven. He said, "To think of it is absurd, because my whole philosophy of life is just very opposite to Jim Jones."[9] Coincidentally, the daughter of Congressman Leo Ryan—who was killed at Jonestown—was a sannyasin and lived at Rajneeshpuram.

Conflict between Rajneeshees and local residents escalated when the sect attempted to dominate Wasco County elections. Rajneeshpuram's leadership, led by Sheela, initiated the purportedly humanitarian Sharing-A-Home program. In 1984, thousands of homeless people from all across the country were bused in to Rajneeshpuram with the promise of "a clean, warm place to stay, and three meals a day."[10] To most locals, it was evident that the true motive for this seemingly altruistic move was to pad the voter rolls and seize control of Wasco County. "Their philosophy has never been sympathetic to the poor or homeless," said Wayne Fawbush, a member of the Oregon House of Representatives. "Now they've suddenly had a change of heart, coincidentally a month before our election."[11] In response, state and county officials took the unprecedented step of conducting mass voter registration checks on all new applicants. Oregon Secretary of State Norma Paulus assigned a fleet of lawyers to interview each potential voter to determine whether or not they were true residents. In the end, the Rajneeshees' efforts to influence the elections came to nothing, and within weeks, hordes of previously homeless people were evicted from Rajneeshpuram. The Salvation Army ended up spending more than $100,000 taking care of them and providing them with the means to travel back to where they had come from.

The cult then came under fire from the Immigration and Naturalization Service (INS), which began to question the immigration status of the many foreign nationals living at Rajneeshpuram. The Rajneeshees in question responded by conducting mass weddings to

American citizens. The INS refused to fall for this scam, and a host of legal actions followed. By now, much of Oregon strongly opposed Rajneeshpuram, and citizens complained to the governor that the Rajneeshees were an "alien cult." A sign on the road to Rajneeshpuram read, "Better dead than red!" Pictures of Bhagwan Shree were posted, accompanied by the words, "Wanted—Dead or Alive."

The office of Oregon's Attorney General started an investigation into the legal status of Rajneeshpuram, threatening the community's very existence. Increasingly gripped by a combination of persecution mania and megalomania, Sheela responded to criticism from the media with sarcastic defiance that gained her more and more public attention. In one appearance, on the ABC TV news show *Nightline,* she predicted that in a hundred years the state of Oregon wouldn't exist, but the City of Rajneesh would flourish. Statements such as this only served to fuel opposition to Rajneeshpuram.

Behind the scenes, Sheela was preparing to act on her words in the most ruthless way. A group from her inner circle was dispatched to literally immobilize potential voters in the upcoming 1984 Wasco County elections by poisoning salad bars at a number of local restaurants in The Dalles with salmonella, cultured at a secret lab at Rajneeshpuram.

Cited as the US's first-ever bioterrorist attack, 751 diners fell ill with food poisoning, 45 of whom were hospitalized. Shortly afterward, Sheela and her cohorts drew up a hit list of nine people, including US Attorney Charles Turner and Oregon Attorney General David B. Frohnmayer. She anticipated that the murders would derail a federal grand jury investigation into immigration fraud. Sheela and three other Rajneeshees traveled to New York to obtain false IDs, then went to Texas to purchase guns to use in the assassinations. However, at the last minute, reason prevailed, and Sheela called off the plot. However, she was less scrupulous when it came to planning the assassination of Rajneesh's doctor, Swami Devaraj, whom she blamed for supplying Rajneesh with drugs and turning him against her. Sheela ordered Jane Stork, a.k.a. Ma Shanti B, to inject him in the backside with adrenaline. Miraculously, he survived.

Around mid-1985, the commune, wracked by paranoia, began to fall apart. As allegations of criminal activity intensified, Sheela resigned from her role as secretary and fled to Europe with her closest allies. Two days later, Rajneesh broke his three-and-a-half-year-silence to hold an extraordinary press conference, during which he accused Sheela of a number of crimes. He claimed that Sheela—whom he referred to as the "perfect bitch"—and her associates had attempted to poison him, his doctor Swami Devaraj, and the municipal water system at The Dalles.[12] He also claimed that Sheela had planned to crash a plane loaded with dynamite into the Dalles courthouse.

Rajneesh invited the FBI to Rajneeshpuram to investigate his claims. During the investigation, the FBI recovered 200 listening devices (Rajneesh insisted that Sheela had bugged his living quarters) from local homes, hotel rooms, and the Rajneeshpuram restaurant Zorba the Buddha. The FBI also found the guns the group had purchased to carry out hits on their enemies. In Sheela's home, they discovered a hidden tunnel leading to the laboratory where the bacteria used in the salmonella attack had been grown. In addition, unshredded documents were found in the city dump that contained incriminating evidence.

David Berry Knapp, a.k.a. Swami Krishna Deva, the mayor of Rajneeshpuram, was one of the only sannyasins to inform on the cult. He gave damning testimony to the FBI in exchange for a lenient, two-year prison sentence. In his testimony, he claimed that the homeless people bused in to Rajneeshpuram were sedated with Haldol-laced beer. He also claimed that Sheela had poisoned her first husband, Marc Silverman (a.k.a. Swami Chinmaya), who had Hodgkinson's disease, in a mercy killing.

In October 1986, Sheela was arrested in West Germany and, in February 1987, extradited to the US, where she pleaded guilty to first-degree assault and conspiracy to commit assault and wire-tapping. She was sentenced to 20 years and fined $470,000, but was released after serving just 39 months. Following her release, Sheela moved to Switzerland. In 1999, she was convicted of criminal acts preparatory to the commission of murder in relation to the plot to assassinate US Attorney Charles Turner. She was sentenced to time served. In 2018, documents originally found in an old abandoned filing cabinet in 1986, came to light that confirmed Sheela's partic-ipation in the mass-poisonings and the assassination plans.

In October 1985, Rajneesh's utopian dream came to an end when he was indicted on charges of immigration fraud. Federal agents arrested him in Charlotte, North Carolina, as he was attempting to flee to Bermuda on a private Learjet. Rajneesh pleaded guilty to immigration fraud and was deported to India after entering an Alford Plea (effectively pleading guilty) and being fined $400,000. When "the blessed one" returned to India, Rajneesh-puram quickly collapsed and the Rajneeshees there dispersed. Nevertheless, most sannyasins, both in the US and India, continued to accept Rajneesh as their spiritual leader and attributed blame for all criminality associated with the group to Sheela and other members of her inner circle.

At least 42 of Bhagwan Shree Rajneesh's followers were charged with various crimes, ranging from wiretapping to attempted murder. Filipina nurse Dianne Yvonne Onang, a.k.a. Ma Anand Puja, who had total authority over Rajneeshpuram's medical facilities, was sentenced to four and a half years for her part in the mass poisoning in The Dalles.

After the commune disbanded, Rajneeshpuram became a ghost town. In 1996, it was purchased by Montana billionaire Dennis Washington with the intention of turning it into a destination resort. However, he ran into zoning problems and had to abandon the project. The property was then donated to the Christian organization Young Life in 1998. Renamed Washington Family Ranch, it is now the largest Young Life camp.

Rajneesh moved back to his cult's commune in Pune, renamed himself "Osho," and rebranded his sect the Osho Movement. At the entrance to the commune was a sign that read, "If you are coming, you must bring an AIDS test certificate that is no older than one month." Rajneesh believed AIDS was the disease the 16th-century French astrologer and seer Nostradamus was referring to when he said a deadly epidemic would cover the Earth.

On January 19, 1990, Osho, otherwise known as Bhagwan Shree Rajneesh, died from heart failure aged 58. His followers celebrated his "spirit's release" with songs and dancing. His body was taken to a riverside funeral pyre, where it was cremated in traditional Hindu fashion. Many of his followers alleged that he was poisoned while in an American jail. The *Illustrated Weekly of India* suggested that he was poisoned by his own followers. His epitaph read, "Never born, never died; only visited this planet Earth between December 11, 1931, and, January 19, 1990." Despite his early death, Rajneesh's philosophy and teachings live on; hundreds of thousands of people still practice meditation techniques that he taught.

The story of Rajneeshpuram remains one of the most bizarre chapters in the history of Oregon. Aside from the crimes committed by the group's leadership, the case raised issues over the rights of American citizens, according to the US Constitution's First Amendment, to worship and assemble without government interference. Even today, how much Bhagwan Shree Rajneesh knew about the criminal activity at Rajneeshpuram is open to debate. It is largely accepted that it was the abuse of power by Ma Anand Sheela that ultimately led to the self-destruction of Rajneeshpuram; however, some consider that Rajneesh was the mastermind and Sheela was quite simply a scapegoat.

---

[1] *The San Francisco Examiner*, October 13, 1982—"Controversy Follows the 'Sex Guru' West"

[2] *Osho Rajneesh and his Disciples: Some Western Perceptions* by Harry Aveling

[3] *The Laughing Swamis: Australian Sannyasin Disciples of Swami Satyananda Saraswati and Osho Rajneesh* by Harry Aveling

[4] *The New Yorker*, September 29, 1986—"Rajneeshpuram"

[5] *Gurus in America* by Thomas A. Forsthoefel and Cynthia Ann Humes

[6] *The Coeur d'Alene Press*, August 12, 2018—"Guru Rajneesh Brought Cult to Oregon, Poisoned Locals and Promoted Free Love"

[7] *Billionaires Newswire*, February 2, 2015—"The Cult Leader with 100 Rolls-Royces"

[8] *The Golden Guru* by James S. Gordon

[9] *Albany Democrat-Herald*, November 6, 1984—"Rajneesh Says Jonestown Not Possible at Commune"

[10] *Arizona Republic*, November 11, 1984—"Life Inside Rajneeshpuram As Seen By Undercover 'Street Person'"

[11] *The Miami Herald*, October 3, 1984—"Guru Offers Homeless New Life Out West"

[12] *Wild Wild Country* (2018), directed by Maclain Way and Chapman Way

The Family

Glamorous and charismatic, Anne Hamilton-Byrne hoodwinked her followers with drugs and tricks. Claiming to be Jesus reincarnated, she presided over a harsh regime riddled with cruelty and child abuse.

––––––––––

"She captivated me with her talk of things spiritual, her knowledge of God, a familiarity with things psychic, and her soothsaying."

George Ellis, former cult member

––––––––––

Anne Hamilton-Byrne had peroxide blonde hair that she wore in waves and a penchant for cosmetic surgery. She wore expensive perfume and pearls. She also claimed to be Jesus, reborn as a woman. Over the course of two decades, her doomsday cult, The Family, lived in almost complete secrecy, hidden away in the outback near Melbourne, Australia. Aptly, their motto was "unseen, unknown, unheard"—and so they remained, until their crimes were finally brought to light.

The first of seven children, Anne Hamilton-Byrne was born Evelyn Grace Edwards in Sale, a one-road farming settlement approximately two hours east of Melbourne, on December 30, 1921. Mental illness ran in the family. Her mother, Florence Louise, originally from Wandsworth, south London, England, suffered from paranoid schizophrenia; her father, Ralph Vernon Edwards, was an itinerant, possibly suffering from posttraumatic stress disorder from fighting in World War I. Her mother was committed to a psychiatric hospital after setting her hair on fire in the street, spent 27 years in various hospitals, and ultimately died in one. Her father vanished for long periods of time. To avoid repaying a debt, he went on the run and, by the time Evelyn was three years old, was living in a fishing port on Australia's west coast. Evelyn's aunts were institutionalized in Britain, and her sister was admitted to a psychiatric hospital in Brisbane after suffering a nervous breakdown.[1] As a result of all this upheaval, Evelyn spent much of her childhood in the Melbourne Orphanage.

Aged 20, Evelyn Edwards, who had changed her name to Anne Hamilton, married her first husband, Lionel Wale Harris in 1941. They had one daughter named Judy, but tragically, Lionel died in a car accident in January 1955. Throughout their marriage, Anne suffered a number of miscarriages and—a chilling harbinger of what was to come—she and her husband were planning to adopt a baby girl shortly before his death.

Soon after, Anne took up yoga—the study of which was still in its infancy in the Western world—joining a class run by Margrit Segesman, one of the first European yoga teachers in Australia. By now, Anne was telling people that she was working as a physio-therapist. Anne had practiced as a physiotherapist, but there was no record of her ever training as one. She also knocked 10 years off her true age. During this period, Anne became attracted to Eastern religions and mysticism and was thrown out of yoga class for allegedly putting a "spell" on a fellow student, causing him to be sick.[1] "She tried all sorts of things, like the occult," Segesman recalled drily.

During the 1960s, Anne began to teach a yoga class at the Railway Institute Hall in Geelong. Her students were mostly middle-aged women from Melbourne's middle class. "Anne was apparently a wonderful teacher, and these women became her first devotees," observed Chris Johnston and Rosie Jones in their 2016 book *The Family: The Shocking True Story of a Notorious Cult*. Anne tapped into the decade's particular interest in spiritualism and encouraged a number of women to leave their husbands to follow her on a spiritual journey. Divorce was frowned upon at the time, and "[Anne] knew that if she could get them to leave their husbands, their families would disown them—she'd have them for life," said Barbara Kibby, a student in Anne's yoga class. Anne also attracted a number of gay male followers, claiming she could offer them a refuge from Australia's strict laws against homosexuality.

To ramp up her status as a guru, Anne claimed she was the reincarnation of Jesus Christ and that she had reached nirvana and then returned to Earth to help others achieve heavenly bliss. She also told her followers, who called her "The Living Master" or "The Teacher," that she was descended from French aristocracy and owned castles in Europe.

After garnering a great deal of attention in the yoga community, Anne developed The Family—originally named the Great White Brotherhood—in 1963, claiming that she was acting on orders from God. Early on, she won over Dr. Raynor Johnson, an eminent physicist and respected author who was Master of Queen's College at Melbourne University. Anne recruited Dr. Johnson after a brief marriage to Queen's College gardener and caterer Michael Riley and obtaining information about Johnson from him. Armed with this information, she pretended she was clairvoyant, and Dr. Johnson became convinced of her powers. He became Anne's right-hand man in her quasi-religious cult and, as the face of the cult, provided her with a valuable commodity: respectability. Anne remained the cult's dominant force, however. In 1964, she and Johnson bought land in Dandenong Ranges, forested hills near Melbourne, where The Family would live.

At the time, spiritualism was gaining traction in scientific and medical circles. Anne preached a hodgepodge of Christianity,

Eastern mysticism, and apocalyptic prophecy, informing followers that the more difficult their lives were, the better it would be for their souls in the afterlife. She also had an interest in the occult, claiming to have held séances during which she had contacted the spirit of the author and spiritualist Sir Arthur Conan Doyle, creator of Sherlock Holmes. Unexplained UFO activity, mysteriously cited by Anne as "a warning," was also incorporated into her belief system.[2]

Johnson's air of authority helped Anne to collect acolytes from Melbourne's wealthy, educated elite, including doctors, lawyers, psychiatrists, and nurses. "I've been waiting for you," Anne would say on meeting a potential follower for the first time. "You are special." Early on, The Family funded themselves through yoga classes and donations made at services held at the chapel on their property in the Dandenong Ranges. In time, however, the cult amassed a vast fortune through property, land, and cash donated by followers. By 1970, members were also obliged to give up a tenth of their income.[3] Anne lived a life of luxury, with homes in Britain, Hawaii, and New York. To maintain the illusion of possessing perpetual youth, she underwent a number of cosmetic surgeries. She also started calling herself Anne Hamilton-Byrne, following a relationship with British businessman Bill Byrne, whom she married in 1978.

The first children of The Family started to arrive in the late 1960s. At the time, adoption in Australia was poorly regulated, and becoming pregnant while unmarried was widely stigmatized. Throughout the late 1960s and 1970s, Anne Hamilton-Byrne collected 28 children through false adoptions thanks to her network of followers, many of whom were in medical or related professions. Unwed mothers—after being scrutinized for racial "purity"—were convinced by a network of cult doctors, midwives, and social workers that their children were either mentally or physically deficient. They were then persuaded to sign their babies over to The Family; lawyers belonging to the cult would falsify the adoption papers. Other children were "given" to Hamilton-Byrne by cult members. One such child was Ben Shenton, who was handed over to Hamilton-Byrne at the age of 18 months by his mother, Joy Trevallyn. According to Shenton, Hamilton-Byrne targeted vulnerable people who were "divorcees, had marriage breakdowns, or who had lost a child."[4] After obtaining the children, Hamilton-Byrne would legally change their names and claim they were her children by birth.

Once the children began to arrive in The Family, Hamilton-Byrne claimed that the apocalypse was imminent but that she and her followers would survive doomsday because they had been chosen to become a new master race. In a bid to create a perfect Aryan race, she bleached most of the children's hair blonde, gave them similar haircuts, and dressed them identically.

The children were kept isolated from the outside world in an old vacation home on the shores of Lake Eildon in the foothills of the High County, around two hours away from Dandenong Ranges. The property had been sanctioned as a home tuition center by the Education Department. Here, the children were supervised by female cult members known as "aunties," who were tasked with educating and raising them. The children were indoctrinated with Hamilton-Byrne's ideas and believed that she was the reincarnation of Jesus Christ, as well as their mother. The home was decorated with photographs of Hamilton-Byrne, and the children were told that she possessed psychic powers, could see them if they misbehaved, and that if they tried to escape, she would kill them.[5] Life in

Lake Eildon was dire, and the "aunties" were physically and mentally abusive toward the children. "They were mean. They starved us. They beat us," recalled Leeanne Creese, who lived in the cult from birth to the age of 17.[6] Hamilton-Byrne beat the children with a stiletto shoe for the smallest disobedience. In addition to beatings, children were punished by having their heads held underwater.

The aunties blindly obeyed Hamilton-Byrne's orders; she would call them at Lake Eildon in order to listen to a beating through the telephone line. In addition to being starved of love and interaction with the outside world, the children were starved for days for minor transgressions. Sometimes children would be so hungry that they raided trash cans and ate leaves and grass. Befitting the cult's motto, children at Lake Eildon truly were "unseen, unheard, unknown."

Hamilton-Byrne demanded total obedience and dictated every aspect of her followers' lives. She told them what to wear and what to eat. She ordered some followers to be celibate; others she partnered up and ordered to procreate. Members accepted their role within the community because they believed that Hamilton-Byrne was "the very center and soul and substance of the way of salvation laid down by the supreme father." They believed that when Hamilton-Byrne invited them to become a disciple, she took over the administration of their karma. The cult strongly believed in reincarnation and that they had to follow the spiritual path Hamilton-Byrne laid before them. To further their belief in reincarnation, Hamilton-Byrne kept a large number of cats; she claimed they were people who had died and returned to Earth in feline form. Some members feared that if they disobeyed Hamilton-Byrne, they could end up in the cat kennel. When a cat died at

Lake Eildon, Anne Hamilton-Byrne would set up a macabre memorial in one of the children's bedrooms and they had to sleep with the decomposing animal.[7]

Hamilton-Byrne also forced her followers—children included—to take LSD or magic mushrooms as part of their initiation. They were injected with the drug and then left in a darkened room for several days. While they were in this vulnerable state, Hamilton-Byrne would appear at the door in a flowing white gown. A bucket of dry ice placed behind her provided extra spooky atmosphere. According to Hamilton-Byrne, the purpose of these antics, which she referred to as "clearings," was to take members back to their past lives to discover what had made them unhappy. In reality, however, hallucinogenic drugs were used to reveal psychic weaknesses and to ensure that followers accepted Hamilton-Byrne's divinity. One of her early acolytes was psychiatrist Dr. Howard Whitaker, a researcher in the use of psychedelics to treat mental illness. Whitaker supplied drugs, which were then administered to cult members by psychiatrists, nurses, and sometimes Hamilton-Byrne herself. Several children who grew up in the cult later claimed that, while under the influence of LSD, they were forced to have sex. Before being introduced to LSD, children were variously drugged with Mogadon, Largactil, and Valium to keep them docile.

From the 1960s until 1982, Hamilton-Byrne and a group of cult psychiatrists tested LSD on patients at Newhaven Private Hospital, located in Kew, claiming they were conducting mind control experiments. More than 100 patients were experimented on, and Dr. Whitaker documented his results in the group's "Medical Journal." He said that the "treatment" was aimed to use the patient's altered state of consciousness to speed up their responses to psychotherapy. These experiments were allegedly jointly sponsored by the Canadian Government and the CIA. A number of these patients were later recruited into the cult. "She captivated me with her talk of things spiritual, her knowledge of God, a familiarity with things psychic, and her soothsaying," said George Ellis, a former member of The Family.[7] Cult "clearings" were occasionally held at Newhaven Private Hospital, where Family members were admitted as fee-paying patients. "Clearings" were arranged by Hamilton-Byrne for various reasons; for example, two men were injected with LSD because she said they had "sewerlike minds" after they commented on a mini-dress she was wearing. Until 1975, LSD was provided through the Health Department to psychiatrists. However, when it later became more difficult to obtain, Hamilton-Byrne created a concoction using the juice from peyote cacti. As Hamilton-Byrne had control of a psychiatric hospital, followers were afraid to question her; she often threatened that it only took two psychiatrists to involuntarily commit somebody.

Hamilton-Byrne first came to the attention of the authorities in the early 1980s following the disappearance of 10-year-old Kim Halm, the daughter of a former cult member named Hans Halm, who had changed his name to George Ellis. When he had left the cult he had also left his daughter, wife, and two children Hamilton-Byrne had ordered the couple to adopt. Ellis hired Melbourne private eye Barbara Palmer to investigate his daughter's disappearance. In 1981, Palmer received an anonymous tip that children were being held captive at Kai Lama, a.k.a "Uptop," The Family's base at picturesque Lake Eildon. While Palmer couldn't get very near the property, she managed to take photographs of the children in the garden before they were ushered inside by the aunties. It was a peculiar sight: virtually indistinguishable children with peroxide bob cuts and similar outfits. The pictures led to the property being raided by the police. However, probably thanks to a tip-off, all the officers found was "Thirteen to fourteen kids, well-dressed, well-behaved, and having a birthday party." Believing nothing was awry, no further action was taken.[8] (Kim Halm was subsequently found to be living with her mother in Auckland, New Zealand.)

The Family was left undisturbed until 1983, when Melbourne newspaper *The Age* ran a series of articles on the cult. In their wake, Victoria Police's Delta Taskforce recommended that the cult should be investigated for child exploitation. However, a senior police officer claimed this was unwarranted and denied the investigation.[9]

After years of rumor and speculation about the cult's activities, police finally raided The Family's Lake Eildon property on a warm summer morning in August 1987. The raid that PI Barbara Palmer had been waiting for "for six long years," according to *The Sydney Morning Herald*, was prompted when Sarah Hamilton-Byrne, 17, Anne Hamilton-Byrne's daughter, fled the cult, stirring the Community Policing Squad into action. Police rescued seven children, freeing them from a life of deprivation and seclusion. However, a lack of physical evidence led police to declare that abuse could not be substantiated. Therefore, several aunties only faced charges relating to welfare fraud. Anne Hamilton-Byrne, her husband Bill—whom an ex-follower once described as "a handsome, rich, compliant handbag"—along with several cult children, fled overseas.[2]

When The Family first formed, Australian society largely dismissed the cult as a harmless group of yoga fanatics. This misconception remained until The Family's disturbing practices were laid bare for Australia and the world to see. Many followers were left with psychological scars that lasted the rest of their lives. The combined effects of prolonged doses of LSD and enforced isolation proved traumatic for a number of children who, as adults, suffered personality disorders, depression, recurring nightmares, and social withdrawal. Some even incurred permanent brain damage, while one was left with only 10 percent vision. By 1990, it was reported that at least five members of The Family had committed suicide. One jumped from a bridge in London, one drank weed killer, one hanged himself in a psychiatric hospital outbuilding, and two more died from drug overdoses. [10] That year, survivors of the Newhaven Hospital LSD experiments shared a $750,000 out-of-court settlement paid by the CIA.

After an extensive investigation—known as Operation Forest—involving police in Australia, the UK, and the US, Hamilton–Byrne and her husband were arrested at their home in the Catskill Mountains, New York, on June 4, 1993. When arrested, they had 30 dogs and 70 cats.[11] The couple were extradited to Australia, and in November, they pleaded guilty to conspiring to make false statements in registering the births of three children and fined AU$5,000. Hamilton–Byrne and her husband then dropped out of the media spotlight. In the few interviews she gave, she claimed she was innocent and had never been a cult leader. In 2010, Hamilton–Byrne developed dementia and was sent for palliative care to a Melbourne nursing home. She died, aged 97, on June 13, 2019, having never served time in prison.

---

[1] *The Age*, September 8, 1990—"From Orphanage to $50m Guru"

[2] *The Family: The Shocking True Story of a Notorious Cult* by Chris Johnston and Rosie Jones

[3] *The Age*, September 11, 1990—"The Family Spreads Out"

[4] News.com.au—August 21, 2018—"Children of the Damned: How My Mother Gave Me to a Sinister Cult as a Baby"

[5] *Unseen, Unheard, Unknown* by Sarah Hamilton-Byrne

[6] CBS-6 WTVR, April 29, 2017—"The Family Cult"

[7] *The Age*, September 13, 1983—"My Daughter Is at Eildon Centre, Says Former Cult Man"

[8] *The Sydney Morning Herald*, August 22, 1987—"Sect Exposed by Private Eye"

[9] *The Age*, September 24, 1994—"Children Celebrate Release But Little Else"

[10] *The Age*, September 1990—"The Family and Its Use of Drugs"

[11] *Bizarrism* by Chris Mikul

The Narcosatanists

The murder of 21-year-old student Mark Kilroy revealed the horrifying crimes of the Narcosatanists cult, who practiced black magic involving torture, ritual murder, and human sacrifice to further their drug-smuggling operations.

"The sense of evil was tangible. You could feel it. You could sense it. You could certainly smell it because the whole place reeked of death."

Dr. Tony Zavaleta, anthropologist specializing in Mexican folklore

---

One of the most gruesome and bizarre tales of evil in the history of the Rio Grande Valley unfolded in 1989, with the disappearance of 21-year-old American student Mark J. Kilroy, offered up as a human sacrifice to voodoo spirits by a drug-smuggling cult known as the Narcosatanists. The cult's leader, Adolfo de Jesus Constanzo, and his girlfriend, Sara Aldrete, used a combination of charm and intimidation to induce their followers to commit appalling acts of torture and depravity in the name of Palo Mayombe, a perverted form of the Santeria religion.

Adolfo de Jesus Constanzo was born in Miami, Florida, on November 1, 1962, to a 15-year-old Cuban immigrant. Constanzo was raised in Puerto Rico, where his mother, Delia Aurora Gonzales, married for a second time. When his stepfather died, he and his mother returned to Miami, purchasing a house on Coral Park Estates in West Dade. As a young boy, Constanzo accompanied his mother on trips to Haiti to learn about voodoo and black magic. Gonzales came to believe her son would become the greatest-ever practitioner of black magic. With the aid of a Haitian "godfather," Constanzo was taught the finer points of black magic. He was also sexually assaulted.[1] Back in Miami, the family followed the Santeria religion and practiced animal sacrifices at their suburban home. Neighbors recollected seeing headless chickens, geese, and goats strewn across their garden. If someone crossed Gonzales, they could expect to find a decapitated animal on their doorstep. Inside, the home resembled a slaughterhouse; floors were dotted with excrement and blood spattered the walls, while the next animal to be sacrificed wandered aimlessly amid the chaos.

According to Gonzales, Constanzo started having out-of-body experiences and visions when he was a teenager and could allegedly heal the sick and predict the future. As an adult, Constanzo came to believe that only by embracing absolute evil could absolute power be achieved. In 1984, the opportunities for making big money in the drug trade took him to Mexico. He realized that superstitious Mexican drug lords would turn to him for his magical protection, convinced that this would enable them to conduct their business undetected.

Constanzo's "magical powers" gained him entrance to the highest levels of Mexican society and also provided him with police contacts. Wealthy, influential citizens paid him thousands of dollars for a prediction and a *limpia*—a traditional Mexican spiritual cleansing ritual—which Constanzo claimed brought good luck and healing to those cursed by their enemies. Constanzo also sought out drug dealers and offered them protection from the law with one of his concoctions in return for a generous cut of their profits. He claimed that his magic spells were responsible for a drug cartel's success and that his powers could bring his clients great wealth, as well as vengeance against their enemies. Before long, Constanzo found himself the leader of a small gang of drug smugglers based in the city of Matamoros, conveniently located on the US-Mexican border. Constanzo and his gang—which included the Hernandez brothers, members of a notorious drug-smuggling family—became major players in the marijuana trade, shipping the drug from farms to Rancho Santa Elena, the gang's ramshackle hideout near Matamoros. From there, it was smuggled into the US via the Rio Grande River, the border that separates Brownsville, Texas, from Matamoros, Mexico. Constanzo ruled his followers with a mix of fear and cold, hard cash. His apparent links to the powers of darkness made his followers obey him unconditionally. In addition, Constanzo provided his followers with more money than they could have dreamed of.

Constanzo and his followers practiced a form of witchcraft in which animal and human parts were used in rituals to ward off evil spirits and provide a "magical shield" from detection by police. Their practices derived from the religious tradition of Palo Mayombe. Like its better-known counterparts, Voodoo and Santeria, Palo Mayombe is an Afro-Caribbean religion brought to the islands by slaves hundreds of years ago. Constanzo's Narcosatanist version, perhaps derived in part from the 1987 movie *The Believers*, included ritual human sacrifice, despite the fact that this had not been part of Palo Mayombe belief for hundreds of years. When a new sacrifice was required, Constanzo ordered his followers to abduct someone from the street. Usually, the victim would belong to a rival drug-smuggling gang. The victim would be bound and blindfolded and taken to Rancho Santa Elena; there they would be tortured, sodomized, castrated, beheaded, and dismembered. Constanzo believed that it was essential to the success of the ceremony that the victim should experience as much fear and pain as possible. While still alive, victims would be flayed, boiled, and have body parts hacked off. Constanzo would then take parts of their bodies—such as the heart and brain—and place them in an iron cauldron, known in Palo Mayombe as a *nganga*, alongside scorpions, spiders, magic sticks called "palos," and other ominous ingredients.[2] The resulting brew was then passed among members to drink and be sanctified. Constanzo believed that the *nganga* captured spirits, allowing him to speak to demons and to the dead.

A 14-year-old boy, related to one of the cult members, was sacrificed by accident. One of Constanzo's closest associates, Elio Hernandez, grabbed the teenager off the street and promptly decapitated him, apparently without looking at his face. Afterward, he realized the boy was his own cousin.[3]

Constanzo's followers believed that he was the devil incarnate. They nicknamed him *El Padrino*, "The Godfather," and were convinced that he could predict the future. The cult's high priestess was 6 ft 1 in (1.85 m) tall Sara Maria Aldrete, a young woman from a middle-class Mexican family. Aldrete lived an uncanny double life. By day, she was a straight-A physical education major at Texas Southmost College, president of the college's volleyball club, and a recipient of the "Outstanding Physical Education Student" award. "She was the kind of person who always said 'Hi' to you," a fellow student recalled.[4] By night, Aldrete was a "*narcotraficante*," frequently carrying drugs to and from Texas and Mexico. Aldrete, whom Constanzo nicknamed "La Madrina" ("The Godmother"), was his girlfriend, but he also had two male lovers and frequented Mexico City's Zona Rose, a well-known gay neighborhood.

The cult's downfall began in March 1989, when Constanzo ordered his followers to abduct an American with a "superior brain," claiming that "[this] will give the *nganga* more strength to help it think clearly."[5] Twenty-one-year-old American student Mark J. Kilroy inhabited a totally different world to Constanzo and his band of black-magic cultists. Kilroy was a bright premed

Rajneeshpuram

Bhagwan Shree Rajneesh—spiritual guru of Rajneeshpuram or master manipulator?

Free love and primal-scream therapy formed part of Rajneesh's program of self-realization.

Resplendent in one of his fleet of Rolls-Royce's, Rajneesh greets an adoring crowd of his sannyasin followers in the cult's newly built city, Rajneeshpuram.

This aerial photograph gives an idea of the size and scope of Rajneeshpuram.

In Portland, Oregon, sannyasins from Rajneeshpuram in their distinctive orange and red clothes protest against the actions of the Immigration and Naturalization Service.

Rajneesh's secretary Ma Anand Sheela faces the media in 1982.

Rajneesh and followers under arrest in October 1985.

The Family

Anne Hamilton Byrne and her husband arrive at County Court, Melbourne in 1993.

The Narcosatanists

Adolfo de Jesus Constanzo, leader of the Narcosatanists.

Narcosatanist member Alvaro de Leon Valdez is arrested by police in Mexico City.

The grief-stricken parents of Narcosatanist victim Mark Kilroy at a memorial service for their son.

Five captured Narcosatanist gang members stand behind a table loaded with cult paraphernalia. Coleader Sara Aldrete is on the far right.

Sara Aldrete in jail for her involvement in the deaths of 15 people at the Narcosatanists' Santa Elena ranch.

The shack at the cult's Santa Elena ranch where Constanzo enacted his sadistic rites.

Texas Attorney General Jim Maddox views a *nganga* cauldron containing "magical" items at the cult's ranch.

The Kirtland Cult

Jeffrey Lundgren, fanatical leader of the Kirtland Cult, under arrest.

The Avery family, innocent victims of the Kirtland Cult's murderous delusions.

Alice Lundgren, son Damon and husband Jeffrey on trial in 1990.

The Order of the Solar Temple

Luc Jouret, cofounder of the Order of the Solar Temple doomsday cult.

Solar Temple coleader Joseph di Mambro (on left) with cult member Michel Tabachnik.

The wreckage of a farmhouse in Cheiry, Switzerland, where 23 Solar Temple cultists committed suicide.

Ceremonial capes retrieved from a burned-out chalet in Morin-Heights, Canada, another scene of multiple deaths associated with the Order.

The Branch Davidians

Vernon Howell, later David Koresh, with mother Bonnie and younger half-brother Rodger.

David Koresh, his sole legal wife Rachel and their son Cyrus.

Holding a bible, self-proclaimed prophet David Koresh preaches a sermon to his Branch Davidian followers.

The Branch Davidians' Waco compound erupts in flames while besieged by the FBI.

Kiri Jewell, who testified that Koresh had molested her when she was just 10 years old.

IS YOUR CHURCH ATF APPROVED ??

PLEASE DON'T GAS OR BURN ANY MORE CHILDREN

I LOVE MY COUNTRY BUT I FEAR MY GOVERNMENT

Demonstrators protest against the FBI's use of violence to end the 51-day Waco siege.

The siege's tragic outcome also led to protests against government interference in citizens' religious freedoms.

Aum Shinrikyo

Shoko Asahara, founder and leader of the Aum Shinrikyo doomsday cult.

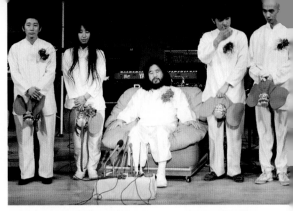

Aum Shinrikyo forms a political party, January 7, 1990.

Aum Shinrikyo followers perform obeisance to Asahara, whom they believed would save them in a coming apocalyptic war caused by the US.

Aum Shinrikyo followers wearing Asahara masks parade in Tokyo, January 20, 1990.

Members of Tokyo's fire department in hazmat suits tackle Aum Shinrikyo's sarin gas attack on the Tokyo metro, March 20, 1995.

Rescue workers help survivors of the sarin gas attack in which 13 people died.

Heaven's Gate

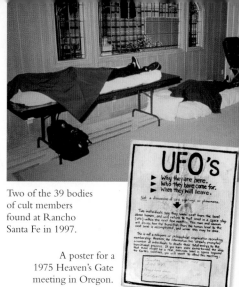

Heaven's Gate leaders Marshall Applewhite and Bonnie Nettles under arrest in 1994 for auto theft and credit card fraud.

Two of the 39 bodies of cult members found at Rancho Santa Fe in 1997.

A poster for a 1975 Heaven's Gate meeting in Oregon.

Movement for the Restoration of the Ten Commandments of God

A soldier views the devastated church of the Movement of the Restoration of the Ten Commandments of God in Kanungu, Uganda, where hundreds of cult members burned to death on March 17, 2000.

NXIVM

An artists' sketch of NXIVM leader Keith Raniere during his trial.

Actress Allison Mack, convicted of recruiting women into NXIVM's sex-slave sorority cult.

student at the University of Texas in Austin who had recently celebrated his 21st birthday. "When he was around, he always lifted people up," his father Jim recalled.

On March 10, Kilroy and three friends, Bradley Moore, Bill Huddleston, and Brent Martin, made their way to South Padre Island near Brownsville to celebrate Spring Break. Each year, thousands of Americans flock across the border to South Padre Island, lured by its beaches, vibrant nightlife, and cheap cocktails and beers. After enjoying the festivities for a few days, on March 13, the group of students crossed the bridge to party in Matamoros, oblivious to the widespread poverty there that breeds violent drug-smuggling gangs. At around 2 a.m. on March 14, the Spring Break crowds in Matamoros began to disperse. Kilroy and his three friends headed back toward the International Gateway Bridge to return to South Padre Island. Kilroy was lagging behind his three friends and, as they approached Garcia's Restaurant, they noticed he had vanished somewhere along Álvaro Obregón Avenue. The trio retraced their steps, hoping to find their friend. Unable to do so, they reported Kilroy missing to the Mexican police.

US and Mexican law enforcement commenced an extensive search for Mark Kilroy on each side of the Rio Grande River. Unbeknownst to those participating in the search, Kilroy had been abducted in a truck driven by Constanzo's followers. When the driver went down a side street to urinate, Kilroy darted out of the door and sprinted for his life. However, another vehicle containing cult members was following behind them. As he ran, the cult members from the second vehicle seized him.[6] Transported to the Rancho Santa Elena, Kilroy was blindfolded, bound, stripped naked, sodomized, and castrated by Constanzo. "Then all of a sudden we heard a sound like when you slice a coconut," cult member

Serafin Hernandez later recalled. "Boom!" Constanzo had cracked Kilroy's head open with a machete. His brain and heart were removed for Constanzo's *nganga* ritual.[7] Kilroy's body was then cut up and buried in the ranch grounds.

For some time, the local police had heard rumors that Rancho Santa Elena was a drug drop-off point en route to the US. The authorities had been alerted, but no action had been taken. (It was later alleged that Constanzo had bribed investigators to turn a blind eye.) Neither had the murders committed by the cult attracted much police attention. However, the killing of a US citizen—a young, good-looking student with all his life ahead of him—would severely impact the local tourist trade, and that was a different matter. Furthermore, Mark Kilroy's uncle held an important position at the US customs office. With US law enforcement heavily involved in investigating Kilroy's disappearance and a $15,000 reward offered for information, the Mexican police set up checkpoints throughout Matamoros, ensnaring a number of drug runners in the process.

Serafin Hernandez was so convinced of Constanzo's magical powers that he believed himself mystically protected from the *federales*. Believing he was invisible, he led police directly to Rancho Santa Elena. He was arrested along with three other cult members: Sergio Martinez, David Serena Valdez, and Elio Hernandez. After violently interrogating them for several days, officers raided the ranch. They were unsure what to expect—perhaps nothing more than a drug haul. Instead, they stumbled across a killing field: the graves of Kilroy and 14 other men, all of whom had been dismembered to fit predug pits. The victims had been blindfolded and killed with a machete or shot. Most had had their hearts and brains removed. A coat hanger had been inserted into Kilroy's spine so that when his body decomposed, it could be pulled from the earth and used as a trophy.

Upon entering a small tarpaper shack on the ranch, the officers staggered back, reeling from the stench of decomposing flesh. Inside, they found macabre evidence of a quasi-religious cult. In a maggot-infested *nganga* cauldron, they came across blood, magic sticks, rum, tequila, bones, a dead cat, parts of scorpions, spiders, and a human brain—apparently that of Kilroy. In several kettles, they found the severed head of a goat, a dead rooster, and a decomposing turtle. Among the paraphernalia of Palo Mayombe, they found bottles of cane liquor, votive candles, pennies, and boxes of cigars. Two blood-stained wires twisted into loops dangled from the roof beam. "The sense of evil was tangible," recalled Dr. Tony Zavaleta, an anthropologist specializing in Mexican folklore who was asked to advise on what had been found at the ranch. "You could feel it. You could sense it. You could certainly smell it because the whole place reeked of death."[8] The evidence found at Rancho Santa Elena, coupled with the confessions of the arrested cult members, steered the investigation toward Constanzo and Aldrete (who, after being tipped off about the raid, had fled to Mexico City).

The cult was now the target of an international manhunt, which lasted until May 6, 1989, when Mexico City police closed in on a dilapidated apartment on Rio Sena Street, where Constanzo and several of his followers—including Aldrete—were hiding out. When Constanzo spotted the police approaching the apartment, he became hysterical and began to throw bundles of money out of the window into the street below, shouting "No one's going to have this money!"[9] Moments later, he grabbed his machine gun and began to fire indiscriminately out the window. Constanzo's talent to manipulate weaker minds served him well, right up to his own death. Rather than surrender or be killed by police, he ordered one of his acolytes, Alvaro de Leon Valfez, to kill him and his right-hand man and lover, Martin Quintana. Constanzo and Quintana entered a flimsy closet in the apartment; Valfez grabbed a machine gun and, obeying his leader's orders, directed a fusillade of bullets at the closet. "[Constanzo] ordered [Valfez] to kill him because it was the end and he wanted to die with Martin," said Aldrete. Moments later, police stormed the apartment and arrested the remaining cultists. In total, 14 members were arrested and charged with crimes, ranging from murder and drug-running to obstructing the course of justice.

Aldrete and the Hernandez brothers were charged with multiple murders and each sentenced to serve more than 60 years. Valfez was sentenced to 30 years. The death of Adolfo de Jesus Constanzo closed the case on the cult. But along the Texas-Mexico border, especially at Spring Break time, the horrific deeds committed at Ranch Santa Elena—"Devil Ranch" in the minds of many— reverberate down the years.

---

[1] *Buried Secrets: A True Story of Serial Murder* by Edward Humes

[2] *Philadelphia Examiner*, April 7, 2012—"Adolfo de Jesus Constanzo 20th Century Killer and Black Magician"

[3] *Texas Monthly*, June 1989—"The Work of the Devil"

[4] *Rolling Stone*, June 29, 1980—"The Believers: Cult Murders in Mexico"

[5] *The Marshall News Messenger*, April 11, 1999—"Spring Breaker's Slaying Remembered"

[6] *Murder Casebook,* part 78—"The Devil's Disciple"

[7] *The Sudbury Star*, March 10, 2007—"El Diablo in Mexico"

[8] *The Monitor*, March 8, 2009—"Lost to the Darkness"

[9] *The Orlando Sentinel*, May 8, 1989—"Cult Boss Ordered Own Death"

The Kirtland Cult

Jeffrey Lundgren was convinced he was God's prophet. His perverse readings of Bible scripture attracted a few fanatical followers and resulted in the horrific murder of an innocent family.

"Some people in the name of God do a lot of crazy things. Jeff used religion for all the wrong reasons."

Rev. Dale Luffman, the Reorganized Church
of Jesus Christ of Latter Day Saints

Kirtland, Ohio, is a rural farming community of around 6,000 residents, located approximately 30 miles (48 km) east of Cleveland. This sleepy hamlet—known as the "City of Faith and Beauty"—is a Mecca to members of the Reorganized Church of Jesus Christ of Latter Day Saints (RLDS), who view Kirtland as the birthplace of their faith. In early January 1990, this quiet little town was swarming with reporters and police officers. It had become the center of an explosive drama that combined power, murder, and religious fervor. Local people looked on in horror as one by one, five bodies—three of them children—were removed from a barn on farmland rented out by Jeffrey Lundgren, the leader of an unnamed cult.

Jeffrey Lundgren was born on May 3, 1950, in Independence, Missouri. He was raised as a member of the Reorganized Church of Jesus Christ of Latter Day Saints, which had splintered from the far larger, Utah-based Church of Jesus Christ of Latter Day Saints—commonly referred to as the Mormons. Both groups trace their roots back to Joseph Smith's inspirational experiences in Palmyra, New York, in the 1820s, and both groups claim Smith as their founder and prophet.

Several former neighbors have attested that Jeffrey Lundgren had an abusive upbringing. The son of a domineering father, Jeffrey was mercilessly teased and harshly punished. His mother Lois was cold toward her son, who felt as though he had to fight for any affection. Jeffrey spent much of his childhood attempting to please his parents and feeling inadequate. Far from giving Jeffrey an inferiority complex, however, this lack of emotional support seems to have led him to develop an abnormal, egotistical need to control others and his environment.[1] He graduated from William Chrisman High School, where he was voted "personality boy," before attending Central Missouri State University.[2]

While studying there, Jeffrey Lundgren met Alice Keeler. Like Lundgren, Alice was a member of the RLDS Church and had had a difficult upbringing, marred by poverty. Her father Ralph suffered from depression brought on by multiple sclerosis and was unable to support the family. Her mother Donna worked long hours as a chef in an all-night café.[3] As a young girl, Alice claimed that she was told by a leader at her RLDS Church that she would marry a prophet of "true greatness."[4] When she met Lundgren, she believed that he was the prophet the leader was referring to and was instantly smitten. A psychologist would later testify that Lundgren and Alice had a common bond: they were both desperately looking for somebody to love them. Alice had been taught that a woman's role was to serve her husband, so when the couple married in 1970, she became his obedient wife, satisfying his every whim. She later claimed that her husband was abusive toward her throughout their marriage, on one occasion beating her so severely that she had to have surgery to remove part of her spleen.

Lundgren spent four years in the US Navy, during which time he and Alice had two sons, Damon and Jason. The young family briefly settled in San Diego, California, but moved back to Missouri when Lundgren was unable to find a job. Here, the Lundgrens had two more children, Kristen and Caleb.

In 1984, Lundgren and his family relocated to Kirtland, Ohio, where Lundgren went to work as a volunteer guide at the Kirtland Temple on Chillicothe Road. The temple—surrounded by trees and manicured lawns—commemorates an 1836 temple built by Joseph Smith Jr. The Lundgren family lived in a church-owned home next door to the temple and also became active participants in the small, red brick RLDS Church across the street from the temple. As part of the church's regular priesthood rotation, Lundgren began to preach; he also taught a Sunday-school class on the Book of Mormon. His traditional views attracted a group of around 30 people who felt that, since 1984—when the RLDS Church officially approved the ordination of women—it had lost its way. Previously, the church had taught that women were subservient to men. A number of Lundgren's followers—Kevin Currie, Richard Brand, Greg Winship, Sharon Bluntschly, Daniel Kraft, Debbie Olivarez, and others who weren't publicly named—were invited to live in his home. Other followers included Ronald and Susan Luff, Dennis and Tonya Patrick, and Dennis and Cheryl Avery, who preferred to maintain their own residences. The members of Lundgren's flock considered themselves conservative, devout Christians who had become disenchanted with the RLDS Church.

Initially, Lundgren appeared to be a devoted worker and teacher but, in the ensuing years, his beliefs and attitudes became increasingly paranoid and aggressive. While Lundgren fit into the basic traditions of the RLDS faith, in that he described visions, spiritual experiences, and prophets, he mostly ignored the Bible's historical context. Lundgren used a system of reading called "chiasmus" to make his own eccentric and dogmatic interpretations of Bible teaching. The chiasmus system involves searching Bible scripture for recurring patterns of words that may then be repeated in reverse order to give diametrically different meanings, as in such phrases as "The first shall be last and the last shall be first" or "The Sabbath was made for Man, not Man for the Sabbath." Because God made Man in his mirror image, it is claimed that God's *own words* may be found between similar-sounding phrases in the Bible and Book of Mormon.

In 1986, Rev. Dale Luffman took over as pastor of the 350-member church, and he soon started to receive complaints about Lundgren. By 1987, RLDS officials started proceedings to revoke Lundgren's priesthood license over concerns that he was preaching radical religious doctrines and also stealing from the church. They discovered that Lundgren had embezzled between $25,000 and $45,000 from temple donations and bookstore receipts. His membership of the church was revoked, he was fired from his tour guide job, and he was ordered to move out of his church-owned home.

Lundgren promptly urged his coterie of followers to resign their church memberships and join him on a new journey. The sect rented a large, derelict farmhouse some 4 miles (6 km) away on Chardon Road, offering to repair the building in lieu of rent. In October 1987, Lundgren and his "family" moved into the farmhouse and developed a communal lifestyle. Lundgren closely supervised his followers, who called him "Dad." He insisted on driving them to and from work and monitored their phone calls, mail, and visitors. Eventually, his followers became isolated from friends and family and were even forbidden to speak to one another in private. Lundgren urged them to sell their homes and turn over all their worldly goods—including any paychecks—to him to pay for group expenses. To keep his adherents hanging on his every word, Lundgren claimed he had sought and received guidance from God. So convinced were they that he was God's spokesman, they granted him absolute spiritual and moral authority. "He was Dad; he was Prophet," said Debbie Olivarez.[5]

At the farmhouse, Lundgren's nightly sermons became progressively more paranoid and apocalyptic in tone. His scriptural interpretations frequently changed. He fed his group a mix of biblical and Mormon scriptures, all of which he interpreted to suit his whims.

By the late 1980s, Lundgren had amassed an arsenal that included numerous weapons and more than 1,000 rounds of ammunition. It was around this time that he told his followers that, in order for them to see God, they first had to seize the Kirtland temple and kill anybody who stood in their way. According to Lundgren, taking over the temple would cleanse the church and pave the way for the Second Coming of Christ, who would establish Zion.[6] In anticipation of the attack, Lundgren's male followers began to wear camouflage clothing and practice with the weaponry they had accumulated. Around this time, followers Kevin Currie and Shar Olson became disillusioned with Lundgren and his violent ramblings and abandoned the cult. They were replaced by Kathryn and Larry Keith Johnson. In 1988, police started to monitor Lundgren and his adherents after receiving complaints of gunfire and paramilitary activity at the farmhouse. In addition, Kevin Currie told police that Lundgren was planning to take over the Kirtland Temple. Police in three separate states were made aware of the cult and their ominous activities but would later claim that they could find no reason to arrest them. For around a year, agents in Missouri, Ohio, and West Virginia exchanged information about the cult but were unable to collect sufficient evidence to build a case against it or its leader.

Meanwhile, Lundgren had changed his mind about seizing control of the temple and, in a misbegotten reading of Mormon teachings, told his followers that they had to perform a blood sacrifice before heading on a quest, where they would be cleansed and search for a "golden sword." According to Lundgren, alongside the sword would be writings containing the wisdom needed to convert the world to the truth of his teaching.[7] Lundgren also declared that the scriptures showed that the worst sin was to keep money for yourself. Based on this, Lundgren said that Dennis and Cheryl Avery were sinful. By this point, the Averys were the only family that maintained some autonomy by living in their own home instead of at the farmhouse. They also kept some of their money for themselves. Although the Averys were loyal to Lundgren, he claimed that they were less enthusiastic than his other followers. He strongly disliked Dennis and abhorred the fact that Cheryl was headstrong. He also claimed that their children—Trina, 15, Becky, 13, and Karen, 7—were unruly. Lundgren insisted that the Averys were lazy sinners and would make a suitable blood sacrifice, referring to slaying them as "pruning the vineyard." The idea of "pruning the vineyard" derived from Lundgren's twisted interpretation of the Parable of the Vineyard in the Bible, in which Jesus claims that all laborers will receive the same reward (in other words, salvation) no matter how long they have worked in the vineyard. "So the last shall be first, and the first last: for many be called, but few chosen . . ."

Lundgren had originally intended to kill 10 people. He based this belief on a passage in the Book of Mormon that stated that 10 people would depart from "the way." Five other members of the cult, along with the Avery family, were targeted for sacrifice. However, after the women had sex with Lundgren, he considered them loyal and "obedient" and spared their lives.

Lundgren convinced his devotees that they had to participate in the murders if they wanted salvation from Armageddon. In preparation, Lundgren had two of his followers dig a grave in a barn on the grounds of the farmhouse. The grave was large, around 6 ft 6 in (2 m) wide and 7 ft 7 in (2.3 m) long—enough to contain a family of five. Lundgren then told his followers—including the Avery family—that they were all going to embark on a camping retreat in search of the "golden sword." Lundgren directed Cheryl Avery to write to family members and tell them the family was moving to Wyoming and would provide contact information once they were settled. This was to ensure that nobody would come searching for them after they were killed.

Lundgren purchased a .45-caliber handgun—using Dennis Avery's credit card—ordered Alice and their three youngest children to stay away from the farmhouse, and set his murderous plan in motion. On the misty evening of April 17, 1989, the Averys were invited to dinner at the farmhouse. After dinner, the women of the cult were instructed to entertain Cheryl and the children while Ronald Luff lured Dennis to the barn on the pretext that he needed help preparing the camping equipment. Lundgren and four of his male followers were lying in wait. On entering the barn, Luff attempted to immobilize Dennis with a stun gun. It malfunctioned, and Dennis was wrestled to the ground and bound with duct tape. "Ow, stop it," pleaded Dennis. "This isn't necessary. Stop. It hurts."[8] His pleas fell on deaf ears. A chainsaw was turned on to muffle the sound of gunshots and, standing in the dim light of the barn,

Lundgren shot Dennis twice in the back and rolled his body into the predug pit. After the shooting, Lundgren's eldest son Damon was the only one who showed any remorse, breaking down in tears. His father ordered him out of the barn to serve as a lookout. Cheryl Avery was then lured into the barn under the pretext that her husband needed help with the camping equipment. She was wrestled to the ground, bound, and blindfolded. "Don't struggle. Just make it easier for yourself," urged Ron Luff. Cheryl was lowered into the pit and shot twice in the breasts and once in the abdomen. Then, in turn, by descending age, the Avery children were escorted to the barn under the pretence of being shown some horses. Seven-year-old Karen was the last to die that night; she had been playing videogames in the farmhouse, completely oblivious that her entire family was being slaughtered. Ron Luff gave Karen a piggyback from the farmhouse to the barn, where she was shot dead. Once all five members of the Avery family were in the pit, it was filled with dirt and rocks; quicklime was sprinkled on top in an attempt to speed up the decomposition process.

The cult said a prayer in the farmhouse, and afterward, Lundgren told his followers that they had impressed him during the blood sacrifice, adding that they'd better get used to it because God was calling for more people to be killed. The following morning, police coincidentally arrived at the house to interview Lundgren about allegations that he was planning a raid on the Kirtland Temple and to investigate reports of improper use of firearms. Police searched the very barn where the murders had occurred but spotted nothing amiss and left.

The cult members hastily packed up their belongings and headed south. Lundgren and his followers traveled to a mountainous area near Davis, West Virginia, where they camped until October. The group kept a low profile; some took jobs, while the rest continued paramilitary training.

Lundgren's weird, tyrannical behavior continued. He declared that the scriptures said he could take more than one wife and that polygamy was God's will. This granted him permission to take Tonya Patrick as a wife. When this arrangement didn't work out to Lundgren's satisfaction, he gave Tonya back to her husband and replaced her with Kathryn Johnson, much to the dismay of her husband, Larry. In addition, Lundgren demanded the women of the cult perform stripteases for him in the woods, threatening to kill their children if they did not comply. Lundgren's disciples finally had enough of his psychotic cruelty. The cult disbanded and the Lundgren family moved to California, while the rest moved to Missouri.

The bodies of the Avery family were discovered during the first week of January 1990, when police were tipped off by Larry Johnson, who hated Lundgren for stealing his wife. The grim discovery set off a nationwide manhunt for Lundgren and his adherents. The following week, Lundgren, Alice, and Damon were arrested by the Federal Bureau of Alcohol, Tobacco and Firearms outside a motel in National City, California. The three other Lundgren children—Kristen 10, Caleb, 9, and Jason, 15—were taken into protective custody. A search of the motel room the family had been staying in turned up an AR-15 semi-automatic rifle, three pistols, and a number of hunting knives, as well as camping and survival gear. Police had decided to check out the hotel after Lundgren made a phone call from a nearby public phone booth to another location that had been placed under surveillance. When the Lundgrens were apprehended, they were just 10 miles (16 km) from the Mexican border. It was thought that they were planning to flee to Mexico and that they had been trying to reach relatives to look after their three young children. The other members of the cult were rounded up in Missouri and, following a series of interviews and interrogations, the truth of what happened on that fateful night in April finally came to light.

The trial of Jeffrey Lundgren began on August 23, 1990. He was unrepentant and resolute in his convictions, professing that he was a prophet and only doing what God had commanded him to do. "It's not a figment of my imagination that I can in fact talk to God, that I can hear his voice . . . All the prophets were commanded to specific acts," he told the stunned courtroom.

Jeffrey Lundgren was found guilty on five counts of aggravated murder and kidnapping and was sentenced to death. He languished on death row for more than 16 years. Having exhausted the legal appeals process, he was executed by lethal injection on October 26, 2006. His last words were, "I profess my love for God, my family, for my children, for Kathy [formerly Kathryn Johnson, now Lundgren's wife]. I am because you are." His last meal was turkey, potatoes, gravy, salad, and pumpkin pie. None of his family visited him in prison during his final 24 hours on Earth. Nobody claimed his body, and he was buried in a prison grave in Chillicothe.

Among those witnessing the execution of Jeffrey Lundgren was US Rep. Steven LaTourette, who served as Lake County's prosecutor at the time of the murders. Also witnessing the execution was Donald Bailey, Cheryl Avery's younger brother. As the curtain in the execution chamber was pulled back, Bailey walked up to the glass window to ensure that Lundgren knew he was there.

The Avery family was buried in Missouri. A church community raised thousands of dollars to pay for their funerals and to launch a children's charity in memory of Trina, Rebecca, and Karen.

Damon Lundgren pleaded not guilty to the Avery slayings. According to Damon, who sobbed intermittently during his testimony, he didn't know about the murder plot until the day the Avery family were killed. "It didn't seem real to me. I was amazed this was going on," he told the courtroom.[9] His defense lawyer argued for leniency because Damon had been raised within a cult and was strictly taught to obey his father. Leniency was denied, and Damon Lundgren was found guilty on four counts of aggravated murder and kidnapping and sentenced to 120 years to life. His mother Alice also pleaded not guilty to the murders, directly contradicting cult members' statements that Alice was directly involved in planning them. She was found guilty on five counts of aggravated murder and kidnapping and sentenced to 150 years to life.

Two of the other men who participated in the murders, Daniel Kraft and Ronald Luff, were found guilty on five counts of aggravated murder and three counts of kidnapping and sentenced to life imprisonment. The remainder of Lundgren's followers received a range of sentences for complicity in the murders. Sharon Bluntschly, Kathryn Lundgren, Susan Luff, Deborah Olivarez, Gregory Winship, and Richard Brand—who participated in the murders but received leniency for testifying against Lundgren—have all since been paroled. Both Dennis and Tonya Patrick were placed on one-year probation for obstruction of justice. The barn where the Averys were killed was razed in 2007, and in its place, the New Promise Church was built.

The Kirtland Cult Killings overwhelmed Lake County's police department, which consisted of just five officers and a chief. Even though Lundgren was no longer affiliated with the RLDS Church, its reputation was seriously tarnished by his cult. "I came to realize the church was as much a victim as the Averys," Rev. Dale Luffman later said. "The RLDS is not the demon here. Some people in the name of God do a lot of crazy things. Jeff used religion for all the wrong reasons."

―――――――――――――――

[1] United States Court of Appeals, Sixth Circuit. *Jeffrey D. Lundgren, Petitioner-Appellant*, v. *Betty Mitchell, Warden, Respondent-Appellee.*
[2] *The Kansas City Star*, August 25, 2006—"Cult Leader to Be Executed"
[3] *End of Days: Predictions and Prophecies about the End of the World* by Sylvia Browne
[4] *Prophet of Death: The Mormon Atonement Killings* by Pete Earley
[5] *The Cincinnati Enquirer*, July 29, 1990—"Trial Focuses on Cult Leader's Control"
[6] *Crime Classification Manual: A Standard System for Investigating and Classifying Violent Crime* by John Douglas, Ann W. Burgess, Allen G. Burgess, and Robert K. Ressler
[7] *St. Louis Post-Dispatch*, January 7, 1990—"Officials Ask Public to Help in Search for Cult Leader"
[8] *Akron Beacon Journal*, August 28, 1990—" 'Stop. It Hurts,' Cried Avery before Slaying"
[9] *The Newark Advocate*, September 17, 1990—"Cult Trial Defendants Face Judges"

The Order of the Solar Temple

Supposedly founded on the high ideals of the Knights Templar, the Order of the Solar Temple was in reality a bizarre vehicle for its leaders' New Age doomsday obsessions. These led, with remorseless logic, to their followers' ritual murder and mass suicide.

"This sect is a secret society so powerful that even the best investigators are powerless to fight it."

Silvio Muller, parent of former cult member

The Order of the Solar Temple gained worldwide notoriety between October 1994 and March 1997, when the bodies of 74 of its members were discovered in various locations in Switzerland, Canada, and France. They were the victims of a planned series of mass suicides and murders perpetrated by Luc Jouret, leader of the Order of the Solar Temple, and Joseph Di Mambro, his chief lieutenant. Before the atrocities made headline news around the world, very few people were even aware of the existence of this small but deadly group.

L'Ordre du Temple Solaire ("The Order of the Solar Temple") was founded in Quebec in the early 1980s by Belgian homeopath Luc Jouret, who was born in 1947 in what is now the Democratic Republic of Congo.[1] When the DRC gained independence from Belgium in 1960, the Jouret family moved to that country. Jouret graduated from the Free University of Brussels in 1974 with a medical degree. He then studied homeopathy, a controversial form of medicine based on the theory that diseases can be cured by giving patients small doses of substances that—in healthy patients—would produce symptoms similar to those of the disease. Jouret also developed a keen interest in spiritual healing and became obsessed with the Knights Templar, the Catholic military order created by French Crusaders in the 12th century. In the early 1970s and 1980s, Jouret established homeopathic practices, first in Belgium and then in France. He was a persuasive speaker and soon attracted a coterie of admirers.

In 1981, Jouret joined the Renewed Order of the Temple, a French right-wing sect inspired by the Knights Templar, and was ordained as a priest. He worked his way up in the organization but left abruptly in 1984 after failing to take over as Grand Master. By now, he had met—and developed a close bond with—Joseph Di Mambro, a shady psychologist who had previously been charged with fraud, breach of confidence, and check fraud.[2] (Di Mambro had actually introduced Jouret to Julien Origas, the founder of the Renewed Order of the Temple.) In 1984, Jouret and Di Mambro founded the Ordre International Chevalresque Tradition Solaire (International Chivalric Order of the Solar Tradition), and Jouret awarded himself the title of Grand Master. In 1986, Jouret and Di Mambro moved to Canada, where they purchased a chalet perched on a hill amid birch trees in Morin-Heights, around 47 miles (75 km) north of Montreal. It was in this picturesque setting that they founded the Order of the Solar Temple.

Over the next few years, Jouret—the Order's front man— lectured on spiritual fulfillment throughout Europe and built up a secret inner circle of followers. Initially, the Order seemed a benign organization that simply encouraged a healthy lifestyle. Admittedly, they had some quirky rituals, such as scrupulously washing with alcohol to avoid cross-contamination and refusing to sit on someone else's seat if it was still warm. The Order also believed that the number seven was symbolic: They washed food seven times before serving it and would repeat gestures seven times.

They believed in New Age philosophies, such as the imminence of the Age of Aquarius, according to astrology, a period of potential enlightenment; they also practiced Druid-style sun and nature worship. Fundamentally, the Order of the Solar Temple believed that they were crusaders for Christ and that their duty was to bring righteousness to the modern world. Cult members had various stages of initiation. Those at the first stage wore white, those at the second wore red, and grand masters wore black.

However, before long, Jouret's lectures began to focus on natural disasters and a coming apocalypse. He claimed that the world was teetering on the brink of ecological catastrophe and nuclear war. In preparation for this Armageddon, the Order stockpiled weapons and built an underground fallout shelter. Jouret tolerated no criticism. He painted a lurid picture of looming catastrophe and held late-night rituals during the full moon, in which he lectured followers on defending themselves and their property after the apocalypse.

Joseph Di Mambro, the Order's coleader and financial mastermind, claimed to possess magical powers and conducted "ceremonies" to demonstrate his abilities. These were nothing more than illusions to fool credulous Order members. Di Mambro and Jouret courted wealthy followers and persuaded them to sell their homes and donate the money to the cult to ensure that they would become part of an elite group destined to survive the apocalypse. Jouret convinced acolytes that when Armageddon came, they would be transported to the star Sirius, where they would live in paradise. However, the only way they could reach Sirius was by "death voyages"—ritual suicide. Jouret also stated that a passage through fire would be the first step on this journey. "He [was] a good talker, charming, and extremely convincing," said Jean-Francois Mayer, a

Swiss historian, adding that Jouret "had the advantage of having the aura of a doctor."[3]

By the early '90s, Jouret and Di Mambro were exerting increasing control over members' lives and becoming more and more secretive about their financial arrangements. Di Mambro had invested much of the cult's money in property, and the organization reportedly owned more than 60 homes around the world. Before long, a number of cultists woke up to the fact that money they had donated was funding the leaders' lavish lifestyles instead of going toward cult projects. Some abandoned the Order, convinced they had been duped—brainwashed into handing over all their money. In 1992, Rose-Marie Klaus sued the Order, stating that it took $500,000 from her and her husband for a farming project. She received a $150,000 out-of-court settlement.[4] The following year, it was alleged that the Order was involved in the illegal arms trade and was backing a right-wing paramilitary group named Q-37. This terrorist group had threatened to assassinate Quebec's Minister of Public Security, Claude Ryan, because of his perceived favoritism toward the indigenous Mohawk people. Despite an extensive investigation, including phone-tapping and raids on cult-owned property, the authorities never found sufficient evidence to charge anyone in the cult, and it is possible that Q-37 never even existed.[5] Following the inquiry, the state-owned power company Hydro-Québec, which had recently suffered attacks on its transmission towers, launched an internal investigation, after it was revealed that several of its employees were members of the Order. The Sûreté du Quebec subsequently arrested several cult members, including Jouret, and charged them with possession of restricted firearms and conspiracy. Jouret himself received a slap-on-the-wrist fine.

When the dust had settled, Jouret moved back to Switzerland, taking a number of loyal followers with him. The Order now viewed all governments as corrupt and decided that they had no alternative but to die as one last statement of their beliefs. In October 1994, they initiated their own form of Armageddon. The first string of deaths commenced with the ritual murder of three-month-old Christopher Emmanuel Dutoit in the Order-owned chalet in Morin-Heights, Quebec, Canada. According to Di Mambro, little Christopher was the Antichrist and had to be killed by driving a wooden stake through his heart. His parents, Antonio Dutoit and Nicky Robinson, were also stabbed to death. The young family was murdered by two other cult members, Joel Egger and Dominique Bellaton, at the behest of Di Mambro. Afterward, Egger and Bellaton fled to Switzerland. Di Mambro's motives for instigating the murders remain obscure. The Swiss police suggested that he had become enraged by Antonio and Nicki Dutoit after they chose the name "Emmanuel" for their son. Di Mambro had a daughter named Emmanuelle and claimed he had fathered her without having sex with her mother, thus gracing his daughter with divine status as the cult's "cosmic child." He allegedly felt that the Dutoits' had committed blasphemy.

The Dutoit family weren't the only ones to die at the Order's Morin-Heights chalet. Two other cult members, Jerry Xavier Genoud and his wife, Collette Emma Genoud, consumed a fast-acting hypnotic drug and then triggered an incendiary device that set the house on fire, killing them both. The authorities were alerted to the crime when family members reported the Dutoit family missing. At the chalet, they discovered the five burned bodies. A plastic bag had been placed over Christopher's head, and he had been stuffed behind a water heater. Two of the bodies had medallions around their necks with the inscriptions T and S, which presumably stood for Temple Solaire, the cult's French name.[6] More horrors were to follow.

On October 5, 1994, residents of Cheiry, a picture-perfect farming village in Switzerland, noticed flames rising from a hillside farmhouse, known as La Rochette, the headquarters of the Order. Volunteer firemen rushed to the scene. The body of La Rochette's owner, Alberto Giacobino, 73, who had rented the house to the cult, was lying on a bed with a gunshot wound to his head, which was covered with a plastic bag. Then, in a room draped with crimson satin wall coverings hidden beneath the farmhouse, the firefighters discovered another 22 bodies—including one child. All of the dead were arranged in a circle and clad in ceremonial robes that indicated their rank in the sect. Most had gunshot wounds to their heads, some had their hands handcuffed behind their backs, and 10 had plastic bags over their heads. According to former cult members, the plastic bags were part of ritual dress to show "how far man had become estranged from his natural state."[7] The room was empty except for a large photograph of Jouret. It led to a small chapel with mirrored walls and an altar in the center. On the altar was a golden chalice, a rose, and a cross. The chapel had been booby-trapped with an incendiary device that had failed to go off; the cult members had intended to exit Earth in a fireball.

Police soon made the macabre discovery that the deaths had been meticulously planned. Almost 100 miles (160 km) south, in Granges-sur-Salvan—a quaint village overlooking the town of Martigny—they discovered two more chalets rented out by the Order had been simultaneously set ablaze. Inside, they found 25 more deceased members of the cult, including four children.[8] Initially, it was speculated that Jouret and Di Mambro had orchestrated the mass suicides and murders so that they could flee with the cult's money. However, a forensic examination of the bodies found at Granges-sur-Salvan confirmed that both cult leaders were among the deceased.

As the world attempted to come to terms with the mass suicides and murders, in December 1995, French police were alerted to the disappearance of 16 missing cult members. While Jouret and Di Mambro had perished in Granges-sur-Salvan, the Order of the Solar Temple had continued to exist. Around 500 police officers searched the snow-capped mountains and remote forests outside Grenoble, France, after members' cars were discovered seemingly abandoned near a skiing center. Sixteen charred bodies were found, arranged in a star-shaped formation around a campfire in a forest clearing known locally as the Pit of Hell. All 16 had taken the sedatives Myolastan and Digoxin before two of the members—Jean-Pierre Lardanchet and Andre Friedli—shot them with rifles before setting their bodies on fire. Afterward, Lardanchet and Friedli committed suicide with Magnum pistols, falling back into the flames as the bullets penetrated their skulls.[9] Among the deceased were three children. Eight of the dead came from Switzerland and eight were from France. Olympic skier Edith Vuarnet, the wife of French Olympic gold medalist Jean Vuarnet, was among the dead. Their son Patrick also died. The cult was so secretive that Patrick wasn't even aware his mother was also in the cult until he reached the "golden circle," the sect's highest rank. Two police officers and a well-known Swiss psychotherapist, Christine Bonet, were also among the dead at Grenoble. Inside the residences of four of the victims, police discovered notes that stated that they were going to "see another world." A few days after the deaths, a number of the victims' relatives and friends formed the Association for the

Defense of Victims of the Order of the Solar Temple to pool their efforts to try and find out what had happened to their loved ones and try to prevent more deaths.

Two years later, on March 23, 1997, five more members of the doomsday cult committed suicide in the village of Saint-Casimir, Quebec. Authorities were alerted to the burning home of Didier Quèze and his wife, Chantal Goupillot, located beside the picturesque river that flows through Saint-Casimir. When the flames were extinguished, police found the bodies of Quèze and Goupillot, as well as Bruno Klaus and Pauline Rioux, in the bedroom. In a scene that was becoming all too familiar, the charred bodies were positioned in the shape of a cross. The Order members had used propane tanks and gasoline to start the fire. The contraptions used to set the homes on fire were extremely sophisticated. A timer connected to a heat source was employed to heat a metal object that, in turn, ignited plastic balloons filled with gasoline.

On the sofa downstairs, they found the body of Suzanne Druau, Goupillot's mother. Similar to the 1994 Order murder-suicides, a plastic bag covered her head. Letters and other documents mentioned that the victims were planning their "departure." Quèze's three children—aged between 13 and 16—were discovered unharmed but heavily sedated in a shed behind the house.

In 2001, Michel Tabachnik, a well-known Swiss orchestral conductor, went on trial in Grenoble for his alleged role in the "assassination" of 14 of the 16 victims. The charges stated that Tabachnik was the third highest-ranking member of the Order and that he had taken part in two 1994 meetings and knew about the deaths but did nothing to stop them. Court documents stated Tabachnik was charged on the basis of evidence that he "edited and distributed doctrinal instructions intended to condition individuals to the idea that they had belonged to an elite with a mission of redemption and to create a dynamic towards murder."[10] Tabachnik's lawyer refuted these claims, stating that his client was the innocent victim of an overzealous justice system. There was clear evidence that Tabachnik was involved with the cult: several members described him as a key cultist, he was present in a photograph of a cult ceremony, and his name featured on a list of cult members found inside the chalet in Morin-Heights. However, involvement in the cult did not mean that Tabachnik was involved in murder and suicide in the eyes of the court. Finding him not guilty, the judge concluded, "The evidence and the cross-examinations have not uncovered sufficient proof, beyond hypotheses, that he had deliberately assisted in the deaths."[11]

Owing to the secrecy of the Order of the Solar Temple, much about the cult itself—the murders, suicides, and motivations—is still shrouded in mystery. It is possible that the deaths were timed to conform to certain astrological calculations. Some commentators have speculated that there may have been more Order of the Solar Temple deaths coinciding with the appearance of the Hale-Bopp comet in 1997.

Some have compared the mass suicides and murders to the Jonestown massacre, but whereas the Order of the Solar Temple followers were well-educated, wealthy, and middle class, those of the Reverend Jim Jones mainly came from the poorer sections of society. It was widely suspected that the Order of the Solar Temple was involved in money laundering. Swiss reports even claimed that $93 million was sent to an account owned by Joseph Di Mambro. However, no firm evidence corroborated these claims. In 1998, the authorities prevented the mass suicide of 32 followers of the Order of the Solar Temple in the Canary Islands. They had believed a spaceship was going to carry them away from the summit of Mt. Teide, a volcano in Tenerife.

While much remains unknown about the Order's workings, what is known is that a shocking majority of its members, in a desperate search for a better existence, were in thrall to not one but two messianic characters. "The leaders of this sect are Machiavellian," said Silvio Muller, whose 43-year-old daughter died in the French Alps near Grenoble. "How can anyone believe that anyone went voluntarily to commit suicide? How can a mother leave her children and kill herself? This sect is a secret society so powerful that even the best investigators are powerless to fight it."

———————————

[1] *The Order of the Solar Temple: The Temple of Death* by Professor James R. Lewis

[2] *St. Louis Post-Dispatch*, October 9, 1994—"Swiss Police Issue Murder Warrants"

[3] *The Times*, October 6, 1994—"Cult Leader Preyed on Wealthy Believers"

[4] *The Toronto Sun*, October 6, 1994—"Cult of Death"

[5] *The Ottawa Citizen*, October 6, 1994—"Cult Was Suspected in Gun Plot"

[6] *Star Phoenix*, October 7, 1994—"Three More Bodies Found Inside Torched House"

[7] *Sunday Tasmanian*, March 26, 2000—"Luxury Temple of Doom"

[8] *Newsweek*, October 17, 1991—"Mystery of the Solar Temple"

[9] *Edmonton Journal*, April 22, 2001—"A Cult's Fatal Attraction"

[10] *National Post*, April 16, 2001—"Conductor on Trial in Cult Deaths"

[11] BBC News, June 25, 2001—"Conductor Cleared of Cult Deaths"

The Branch Davidians

The apocalyptic obsessions of David Koresh, leader of the Branch Davidians, culminated in a showdown in Waco, Texas, with US law enforcement, in which more than 80 people lost their lives. Controversies surrounding this tragedy reverberate to this day.

"I will never forget Waco.

The ghost of Waco will be with me all my life…"

Attorney General Janet Reno

S ituated between the bright lights of Dallas and Austin, Texas, Waco is a quiet, modest city surrounded by sprawling fields and ranches. It had not been the focus of national news since May 1953, when a tornado killed 144 of its citizens. Four decades later, on April 19, 1993, Waco hit the headlines again when the heavily fortified compound belonging to the Branch Davidians, an obscure Christian cult, became the scene of a modern-day Armageddon.

At around 6 a.m., FBI agents moved in to put an end to a siege of the community's compound that had lasted for 51 days and cost several lives. Six hours later, 76 cult members—including 25 children—would be dead after the compound was engulfed in flames. These calamitous events were screened live on television. As viewers looked on in horror, many wondered how so many people could follow the sect's leader, a self-proclaimed prophet calling himself David Koresh, into such a desperate situation.

Koresh was born Vernon Wayne Howell in Houston, Texas, on August 17, 1959. His mother was a 15-year-old girl named Bonnie Clark, while his father—whom he didn't meet until he was an adult—was a young carpenter named Bobby Howell. Too young to provide proper care for her son, Bonnie handed that responsibility to her mother, Erline Clark. When Vernon was five years old, Bonnie reclaimed her son and moved to Dallas to be with her new husband, Roy Haldeman. This drastic uprooting proved traumatic for the boy: "He yelled that she was not his mother and that he wanted to go back," Erline recalled.[1] In school, Howell found it difficult to keep up with the other students, who teased him relentlessly for his learning difficulties. (He was subsequently found to be dyslexic.) Howell suffered another childhood trauma when he was around seven years old, when three older boys attempted to rape him. Howell kept this ordeal a secret until he was an adult.

While Howell failed academically, he displayed a keen interest in religion and a phenomenal ability to learn scripture by heart. By the time he was 13, he had memorized much of the New Testament. A lonely, fervently Christian boy, he would spend hours in his bedroom praying alone and fantasizing about preaching to an eager crowd.

At age 18, Howell joined the Seventh-day Adventist Church in the city of Tyler, Texas. The congregation didn't warm to the autocratic young man, who frequently tried to school them on the Bible. The last straw was when Howell claimed that God had commanded him to take the pastor's 15-year-old daughter, Sandy, as his wife. In 1981, the church voted to disfellowship Howell, and he was swiftly barred. Howell then became involved with the Branch Davidians, a heretical sect of the Seventh-day Adventist Church. The Branch Davidians were founded in 1929 by Victor Houteff, a Bulgarian immigrant and former adherent of the Seventh-day Adventist Church. Houteff left the church after being accused of disrupting an Adventist Sabbath school with his dissident views concerning the coming of God's kingdom on Earth and the future glory of God's people, as prophesied in the Book of

Isaiah, chapters 54–66. The Davidians took the Bible as literal truth—in particular, the apocalyptic Book of Revelation, which culminates in the Second Coming of Christ, the "Lamb of God."

Howell found solace in the Branch Davidians, and it wasn't long before this young, charismatic "Bible expert" had seduced the group's 60-year-old leader, Lois Roden, and displaced her as the groups reigning prophet. This enraged Lois's son, George Roden, who vied with Howell for leadership of the Branch Davidians. The feud between George Roden and Howell intensified when Roden claimed that only one who could raise the dead should be leader. When Roden attempted this feat, Howell reported him to the authorities for "abuse of a corpse," a serious felony in Texas. The Branch Davidians split into two factions. Most members followed Howell to a new base in Palestine, Texas. The unstable Roden stayed at the Mount Carmel Center, the official name of the Branch Davidians compound near Waco. Roden renamed it "Rodenville."

On November 3, 1987, a year after Lois Roden's death, tensions between the two men over leadership of the sect erupted in a gunfight at the Mount Carmel Center, in which Roden received a wound to his hand. Howell and seven of his followers were later acquitted of attempted murder, and state officials had to return a stockpile of weapons they had seized.

In 1989, Roden was convicted of murdering his roommate, whom he claimed had been sent by Howell to murder him. The former Branch Davidians' leader died in a Texas mental institution in 1998.

Howell and his acolytes took over the 77-acre (31.2-hectare) Mount Carmel compound, located some 13 miles (21 km) outside Waco. Closeted in the compound's chapel, Branch Davidians would listen to Howell ramble on for hours without food, sleep, or even bathroom breaks. Howell also had fantasies of becoming a rock star and often played guitar and sang during these meetings.

As the cult's popularity grew throughout the 1980s and early 1990s, people came from as far afield as England, Australia, and Israel to hear Howell's sermons. He urged them to quit their jobs, sell their homes, and move to Mount Carmel—like most cults, the Branch Davidians was largely financed by followers' life savings. Some of Howell's followers were theology students from the Seventh-day Adventist Church from which he had been expelled; others were students from a number of British universities. Diana Henry had been studying for a master's degree when she decided to join. Her father, Sam Henry, recalled, "She was hooked like a fish. She dropped her studies and would have followed this wicked man anywhere. This was the devil's work and she was bewitched."[2] (His whole family eventually followed Diana to Texas, and Sam lost his wife, as well as Diana and four other children in the ensuing April 19 conflagration.)

To outsiders, the Branch Davidians was a quirky but harmless religious group that mostly kept to themselves. Meanwhile, largely cut off from the world, those living at Mount Carmel fell increasingly under the influence of Howell's bullying personality and implicitly violent message. "He had the capacity to discern your emotional weakness and capitalize on that," said David Jewels, the father of a former cult member. "He had this incredible ability to turn your head around."[3]

Howell interpreted prophecies from the Book of Revelation to show that he would die in a battle with nonbelievers who were coming to attack the compound and that this would signal the end of the world. He convinced followers that he was the Messiah and that he would save them—but only if they were willing to die with him. He claimed that his role in the apocalypse was to open the Seven Seals. In the Book of Revelation, only the almighty "Lamb of God" can open the Seals; Howell claimed he now had that power. To underline this assertion, he changed his name to David Koresh. He took his first name from King David, while "Koresh" was Hebrew for Cyrus the Great, the legendary Persian king and conqueror of Babylon who allowed the Jews held captive there to return to Israel and rebuild the temple of God in Jerusalem.

Koresh and his recruiters promulgated the idea that life inside Mount Carmel was safe, secure, and family-oriented. In reality, Koresh destroyed family relationships, ordering children to refer to their parents as "dogs." Children had to urinate and defecate in a chamber pot that was emptied daily. They greatly feared displeasing Koresh, who would punish perceived misbehavior with a wooden paddle called "The Helper."

In addition, whispers of Koresh's predatory behavior started to spread beyond Mount Carmel and out into the real world. Some of these reports may have been exaggerated. Allegedly, Koresh "married" a number of the sect's women, including underage girls. (Koresh seemingly had a particular interest in young girls; he had married his first wife, Rachel, when she was just 14 years old.) Perhaps significantly, the birth certificates of a number of children born at the commune lacked a father's name. Marc Breault, who left the sect in 1989, recalled in the *Washington Post*, April 25, 1993, that child abuse "was quite extensive. And I'm talking about both sexual and physical. Beatings started at an extremely young age— less than a year old. The sexual abuse . . . started at 10 years old."

Koresh told his followers that he had the right to impregnate any woman in order to propagate a race of 24 "perfect" children to repopulate the world after Armageddon. He forced male followers to be celibate, claiming they would contaminate the sect's women with their "imperfect seed." At night, Koresh would enter the women's sleeping quarters in Mount Carmel and choose his conquest for the evening; none of Koresh's followers ever questioned this behavior. Parents even granted Koresh permission to visit their children, fueling his narcissism and messianic convictions.

A slew of ex-members also accused Koresh of claiming he had a mandate from God. A local newspaper, the *Waco Tribune Herald*, launched an investigation into the Branch Davidians and Koresh, running a series titled "The Sinful Messiah" that cited allegations of child abuse, child sexual abuse, and the hoarding of weapons. The newspaper spent eight months reporting on the sect and on Koresh's activities, scouring public records and interviewing a number of former Davidians.

In May 1992, Koresh and the Davidians came to the attention of the authorities after deliveries of more than $100,000 in firearms were sent to Mount Carmel. The sheriff of Waco shared his concerns with the Federal Bureau of Alcohol, Tobacco, and Firearms (ATF). Preliminary investigations uncovered that the sect had purchased M-16 machine-gun conversion kits, commonly used to turn legal, semi-automatic weapons into illegal, fully automatic ones. The sect had also taken delivery of inert hand-grenade casings and black powder capable of charging them. Former cult members came forward to claim that Koresh also had two . 50-caliber rifles that were capable of piercing armor and that he trained followers to shoot to kill. Combined with the claims of underage sex, the ATF was sure there was enough evidence for "probable cause" of criminal activity, and they obtained an arrest warrant for Koresh.

On February 28, 1993, ATF agents left Waco with a warrant for Koresh's arrest and a search warrant for illegal weapons. The ATF allegedly anticipated that their mission, dubbed "Operation Trojan Horse," would be a humanitarian one. However, they arrived at Mount Carmel in an intimidating, 80-vehicle convoy; overhead, two Black Hawk helicopters hovered. The Davidians had been tipped off about the ATF operation and, fired up by Koresh, were in no mood to negotiate.

As was later revealed, Koresh had amassed an arsenal of more than 300 firearms—including illegal machine guns, grenades, and almost 2 million rounds of ammunition—for the apocalypse that he believed was imminent. Shortly after the ATF reached the compound, they were greeted by a fusillade of gunfire—just the beginning of one of the longest gunfights in American law-enforcement history. The ATF was badly outgunned, and the shootout left four agents and six Davidians dead and 16 agents and at least seven sect members injured. David Koresh was shot in the wrist and hip, but his injuries were not life-threatening.

Finally, after three hours of gunfire, a ceasefire was negotiated and the FBI took over operations at Mount Carmel. Nevertheless, Koresh refused to surrender. A 51-day standoff between the Branch Davidians and the FBI followed. During those 51 days of tensions and negotiations, several Davidians managed to escape Mount Carmel, while Koresh agreed to release a steady trickle of children, as well as a couple of women. The followers that remained holed up inside Mount Carmel were now even more convinced that Koresh was God's prophet. During the siege, they held up signs in the windows reading, "Flames Await!" Hoping to break the Branch Davidians' resistance, the FBI played music—including Tibetan chants, Christmas carols, and "These Boots Are Made for Walking" by Nancy Sinatra—at ear-splitting volume. Koresh responded to the pressure by sending out videos in which his followers celebrated him, the Branch Davidians, and Mount Carmel. He even agreed to surrender if a lengthy, taped sermon was broadcast. The FBI complied and broadcast the sermon on radio and television. However, Koresh changed his mind and refused to surrender.

Shortly afterward, Koresh passed three scrawled notes out the front door of Mount Carmel. They were written by Koresh but signed in the name of God. He threatened that catastrophe would befall God's enemies: "Open your eyes and not your mouth. Fear the hour of judgment, for it has come," read one. With no end in sight, the FBI cut the electricity and phone lines in the compound. They also shone floodlights and played loud music in an attempt to unnerve the Davidians and drive them out. When they didn't budge, the FBI bulldozed everything around the compound and surrounded it with wire and armored vehicles. To all appearances, Mount Carmel looked like war zone. In early March, FBI behavioral specialists Peter Smerick and Mark Young warned that these pressure tactics could have negative results and risked pushing the Davidians into feeling they had to fight to the death for their faith. The FBI's onsite commander, Jeff Jamar, told Smerick and Young to refer their concerns to Washington, and he and his aides attempted to increase pressure on Koresh. Smerick soon left the site in frustration at the FBI's aggressive posture. Meanwhile in Washington, after initially rejecting the use of force to end the siege, Attorney General Janet Reno was appalled by FBI reports of beatings and sexual abuse of children being a regular part of life at the Mount Carmel compound.

Finally, on April 19, 1993, Koresh's apocalyptic vision became stark reality. At 5:44 a.m., the FBI telephoned the compound and told Steve Schneider, Koresh's top lieutenant, that they were going to tear-gas the compound unless the cult immediately surrendered. Their threats fell on deaf ears, and Schneider hung up. Minutes later, an armored vehicle moved to the southwest corner of the compound and smashed a large hole in the wall with a battering ram. Another armored vehicle then tore a hole in the second floor and another in the back of the compound. When the vehicles retreated, CS—a powder that stings the skin, eyes, nose, and throat—was sprayed into the large craters while FBI agents fired hundreds of gas rounds through the windows with M-79 grenade launchers. FBI spokesman Bob Ricks said they believed that tear-gassing the occupants was the best way to avert a possible mass suicide because it would cause "mass confusion inside the compound."[4] The FBI expected that the cult members would be forced to surrender. But none did.

Six hours later, smoke and flames spewed from the compound. As fire engulfed the building, onlookers waited in vain for cult members to flee. "I was thinking: Surely they'll come out, surely any minute now we'll see people fleeing," recalled Sarah Sheppard, Waco's tourism director. "It was just one of those things that was a horrible tragedy from all sides and remains with you."[5] It took just 30 minutes for the flames—which were fanned that day by a strong wind—to tear through the wooden buildings, which burned like paper. Nine people managed to escape, but 76 others—including 25 children—died inside the compound. Most of the women and children were found huddled together in a concrete storage area near the kitchen, where they had seemingly become trapped by falling debris and died of smoke inhalation.[6] At least 16, including Koresh, died of gunshot wounds. One boy, who was just 2 or 3 years old, was stabbed to death. Other children were later found to have been shot in the head—part of a mass suicide presumably orchestrated by Koresh himself as a final act of martyrdom. Only four of David Koresh's children survived the siege. By the time the fire department arrived at the site at 12:40 p.m., most of the buildings were gutted.

Ricks subsequently refused to admit the decision not to have firefighters on the scene during the tear-gas attack was a mistake, explaining that the gunfire could have put them at risk.

Nevertheless, repercussions of this judgment traveled all the way from Waco to Washington, where Attorney General Janet Reno claimed full responsibility for using force to end the siege. "I will never forget Waco. The ghost of Waco will be with me all of my life . . . One of the minor tragedies of Waco is we will never know what the right decision was," she said.[7] In the aftermath, ATF director Stephen Higgins and five other high-ranking officials resigned.

In 1994, 11 members of the Branch Davidians were acquitted of murder and conspiracy charges in the deaths of four federal agents. Seven were convicted of lesser charges, while four were acquitted of all charges. The verdict was a serious defeat for the Justice Department and the ATF. The Waco siege sparked a nationwide debate over the rights of groups outside mainstream religions. The raid, the siege, and its grim conclusion were seen by some as unwarranted government intrusion into religious freedom. The FBI—who simply viewed Koresh as a cult leader—were criticized for not fully understanding the religious ideas informing the group. Biblical scholar Dr. Philip Arnold of the Reunion Institute of Houston said that, during the siege, Koresh had asked to negotiate with him but that the FBI had ignored these requests, saying they were just "Bible babble." The ATF was also harshly criticized for the way it chose to execute the arrest warrants; some believed that not enough effort had been made to arrest Koresh away from the compound or to ask him to honor the warrant voluntarily. The ATF replied that their approach was justified, contending that the Davidians had fired the first shot. To this day, there is still much debate over who fired first. Both sides blamed the other.

The Waco siege's horrific outcome haunted all of those involved, and the public was bombarded with conflicting versions of the raid. In July 1995, a congressional hearing was called after a case was made that the FBI had grossly overreacted in their initial raid on the compound and also in the assault on the final day of the siege. "Our goal is to put the facts out before the American people," said Republican Bill Zeliff, co-chairman of the committee. "And find out who's accountable." Lawyers Jack Zimmerman and Dick DeGuerin, who represented Koresh, strongly criticized the FBI, claiming that the organization had rejected Koresh's plan to peacefully end the standoff. The lawyers claimed that the FBI was clueless when it came to dealing with Koresh and his followers. They argued that agents at the scene had agreed to one of the surrender plans put forward by Koresh but were subsequently overridden by "some desk-bound bureaucrat in Washington."[8] Richard Scruggs, an assistant to the attorney general, refuted these claims and argued that the FBI acted in response to Koresh's "lies and misrepresentations." According to Scruggs, the FBI didn't believe that Koresh was ever going to surrender. Attorney General Janet Reno stood by her decision to order the FBI to proceed with the raid: "We all mourn the tragic outcome," she said, "but the finger of blame points in one direction—it points directly at David Koresh . . .The fate of the Branch Davidians was in David Koresh's hands, and he chose death for the men and women who had entrusted their lives to him. And he, David Koresh, chose death for the innocent children of Waco."

During the congressional hearing, 14-year-old Kiri Jewell took the stand and revealed that Koresh had molested her when she was 10 years old. She also said Koresh taught his followers how to shoot themselves properly. "The best way to shoot yourself if necessary . . . was to put the gun in your mouth, back to the soft spot above your throat before pulling the trigger."[6] Fortunately, Jewell's father rescued her from Koresh's clutches just before the initial raid. Her mother—who was one of Koresh's wives—died during the siege.

The question as to the cause of the fire has long been a source of speculation. However, in 2000, a report by a former senator appointed by the attorney general found that members of the Branch Davidians spread fuel throughout the compound to feed the flames. During the siege, 11 bugs, fitted inside milk cartons, were secreted into Mount Carmel by the FBI. One bug captured a conversation between Koresh and Schneider: "They got two cans of Coleman fuel down there?" asks Koresh. "Empty," replies Schneider.[9] In addition to the recording, three surviving Davidians testified that they heard shouts to "start the fire" amid all of the chaos. A team of independent arson investigators insisted that there was conclusive evidence that the Davidians started the fire themselves using flammable fuels in several locations in the compound. The investigation concluded that Koresh was solely to blame, and the jury absolved the federal government of fault. Critics objected, asserting that chemicals in the tear gas, and not Koresh, had ignited the fires. Whatever the truth, David Koresh's prophecies of Armageddon had been fulfilled in the most tragic way. Exactly two years after the end of the Waco siege, on April 19,

1995, Timothy McVeigh perpetrated the Oklahoma City Bombing. The truck bomb, which was detonated outside the Alfred P. Murrah Federal Building, killed 168 people. McVeigh allegedly planned the bombing as revenge for Waco.

The Branch Davidians saga was fraught with missteps on both sides. It also spawned bitter controversies over religious liberty, government force, the right to bear arms, and how such crises should be managed in the future. The siege gripped the nation, offering much for a hungry media: God, the apocalypse, gun culture, sex, rock 'n' roll, mind control, and child abuse. It galvanized antigovernment movements and lone-wolf activists. Even today, some critics insist that federal agents were to blame, while some ever-faithful Koreshians await their self-proclaimed messiah's resurrection.

---

[1] *Austin American-Statesman*, May 2, 1993—"The Making of a Prophet"

[2] *Daily Mirror*, November 2, 2018—"Waco 25 Years On"

[3] *USA Today*, April 20, 1993—"Koresh Ruled with Scripture, Fear, Charisma"

[4] *Associated Press*, April 19, 2018—"The Fiery End of the Standoff in Waco, Texas"

[5] *The Orlando Sentinel*, April 18, 1994—"Memories of Waco Linger a Year After Flames Died"

[6] *Why Waco?: Cults and the Battle for Religious Freedom in America* by James D. Tabor and Eugene V. Gallagher

[7] *The State*, February 27, 1994—"Reno Says Convictions Justify Government Action"

[8] *New York Daily News*, July 20, 1995—"Kid Sex Shocker at Waco

[9] *USA Today*, February 15, 1994—"Waco Tape: Got Coleman Fuel?"

Aum Shinrikyo

Masterminded by a charismatic figure of doubtful sanity, an appalling chemical attack on the Tokyo subway revealed a web of murder and intimidation that rocked Japanese society to its foundations.

_____

"Only members of the Aum will survive Armageddon...

You must devote yourself to Master Asahara;

he is the only one who can save you."

Aum Shinrikyo flyer

_____

Formed in 1984, the Aum Shinrikyo cult began as a harmless spiritual group fusing Hindu and Buddhist beliefs. Matters took a sinister turn when the cult's founder, Shoko Asahara, became obsessed with the apocalypse. The cult amassed an arsenal of chemical, biological, and conventional weapons in anticipation of Armageddon and a final showdown with the government. The attacks perpetrated by Aum Shinrikyo redefined urban guerrilla warfare throughout the world and deeply damaged the long-held sense of safety and security that, up to that time, had prevailed in postwar Japan.

Shoko Asahara was born Chizuo Matsumoto in Yatsushiro Kumamoto, Japan, on March 2, 1955. Infantile glaucoma rendered him blind in his left eye and partially blind in his right eye. The son of an impoverished tatami mat maker, he was sent to a special government boarding school for the blind, only spending holidays with his parents and his six brothers and sisters. Little is known about his upbringing, but it is reported that he showed violent tendencies and an unnatural attachment to money. Because Matsumoto was partially sighted, he was at a distinct advantage over his blind classmates at school, whom bullied and extorted money from.

Matsumoto studied acupuncture and herbal medicine while at school and then, shortly after graduating in 1975, left for Tokyo. According to one of his brothers, he was never close to his family again. He attended a private "cram school" to prepare for college entrance exams that he had previously failed. Matsumoto's ambition was to enter one of Japan's top-ranked schools, but after several rejections, he abandoned his academic plans, married college student Tomoko Ishii, and opened a pharmacy and natural food shop in Chiba prefecture, a suburban district north of Tokyo. In 1982, he was arrested for claiming that a concoction he made from tangerine peel and alcohol could heal rheumatism. He was fined ¥200,000 (approximately $770 in 1982).

Shortly afterward, Matsumoto became the leader of a small group of yoga enthusiasts named Aum Shinsen no Kai, which means "Aum Association of Mountain Wizards." The group traveled to the Himalayas, where Matsumoto met the Dalai Lama (who would allegedly prove an influential supporter of Asahara) and claimed to have reached *satori*—the Japanese term for nirvana. This so-called enlightenment inspired him to change the direction of Aum Shinsen no Kai to a more religion-based group, rebranding them Aum Shinrikyo ("Aum Supreme Truth"). In order to fit in with the new brand, Matsumoto changed his name to the more distinctive Shoko Asahara. He allegedly adopted this name because the number of strokes in its Chinese characters added up to a lucky number. Aum Shinrikyo was a mishmash of Buddhist, Hindu, and New Age teachings. Asahara initially attracted followers by preaching that people were capable of attaining enlightenment through yoga, meditation, and psychic training. Asahara insisted that he possessed extrasensory powers and could levitate, pass through walls, heal the sick, and stay underwater for long periods. Initially, the Japanese government was reluctant to grant Aum Shinrikyo legal recognition. However, it finally became a legal religious organization, following an appeal, in 1989.

By 1990, the cult was a huge success and Asahara had amassed thousands of followers, many of whom lived in the cult's vast compound in Kamikuishiki, a small community of mostly dairy and cattle farmers situated at the foot of Mount Fuji. To his followers, Asahara proclaimed himself to be Jesus Christ and Buddha. In his previous lives, he claimed that he was "King of the Heaven of Degenerated Consciousness" and the ancient Egyptian high priest and architect of the pyramids Imhotep. Asahara urged his followers to abandon their previous lives and families and move to the compound. They survived on an austere diet of rice, vegetables, and "nectar water," which was just regular water that Asahara had blessed by bathing in it. They also turned their property and worldly belongings over to Asahara, who, in stark contrast, ate lavish meals and rode around in a white armored Mercedes . In his 1995 book *Dealing with Criminal Religions: The Case of Om Supreme Truth*, Winston Davis records that members were "thoroughly fleeced," paying out $250 to drink Asahara's bathwater, $11,000 to drink a potion made from his blood, and $100,000 for helmets that allegedly hooked up to his brainwaves. These could also be hired for $10,000 per month.

By 1990, Asahara had amassed substantial real-estate holdings in a number of countries, and it was estimated that Aum Shinrikyo was worth $1.5 billion. His wife Tomoko, according to a 1995 *New York Times* article, was a senior executive. The cult had offices in Tokyo and Kamikuishiki, as well as branch offices in Osaka, Fukuoka, Nagoya, Sapporo, New York, and Moscow. Aum Shinrikyo had particular traction in Russia. It was not proscribed as a terrorist organization until September 2016 and had a membership estimated as between 35,000 and 50,000.

Asahara and 24 followers ran for election to Japan's House of Representatives in 1990. They wore white robes and either elephant masks or Asahara masks and chanted his name in unison. The media was transfixed by this circus and, although the cult was defeated by a landslide, the publicity gained Aum Shinrikyo members. Many of them were highly educated young people, including doctors and scientists who had graduated from Japan's elite universities.

Shortly after Aum Shinrikyo's parliamentary bid, reports of darker aspects of the cult started to emerge in the media. Defectors spoke of forced training that included hard labor and food deprivation. According to these reports, new recruits were forced to undergo "cleansing" whereby they were forced to drink large amounts of water and then vomit it back up. An unnamed female ex-member said that members were forced to take hallucinogenic drugs and locked in underground tombs purportedly to achieve *samadhi*—a yogic state of meditative consciousness leading to enlightenment. The same woman claimed that she was confined in a shipping container for three months after she attempted to escape from the cult's compound in Kamikuishiki. Inside the container, she was forced to watch videos depicting death and mass destruction while an audio recording of Asahara chanting "I am the savior" was played over and over.

An even greater cause for concern were suspicions that Aum Shinrikyo was involved in the disappearance of anticult lawyer Tsutsumi Sakamoto, his wife Satoko, and their 1-year-old son Tatsuhiko in 1989. Aware of the cult, owing to vivid accounts of anguished parents attempting to help their children escape its clutches and from former members attempting to regain assets that they had donated to Asahara, Sakamoto offered his legal services. While investigating these accusations, Sakamoto and his family vanished from their Yokohama apartment on the night of November 4, 1989. There were no signs of violence or struggle, and nothing had been stolen. However, a badge with an Aum Shinrikyo symbol was found on the floor of their apartment. The police suspected the cult's involvement, but no arrests were made.

As the cult grew, Asahara increasingly focused on violent doomsday scenarios derived from the Book of Revelation in the Bible. Asahara told his followers that the US was planning an attack on Japan, turning it into a nuclear wasteland and culminating in a worldwide nuclear holocaust. He also claimed that he had traveled forward in time to 2006 and found out that World War III was imminent. "Four days ago, while on astral plane, I had a vision I was absorbing radiation. I was experiencing the nuclear war that will inevitably occur between 1997 and 2001," he warned his followers.[1] The cult's magazine illustrated the war with pictures of mushroom clouds, tumultuous seas, and raging fires, alongside men in gas masks holding machine guns.

To prepare for the anticipated apocalyptic showdown with the US, a chemical plant was built on the grounds of the cult's compound to mass produce the nerve agent sarin. Originally developed as a pesticide in the 1930s, those who come into contact with the deadly gas salivate profusely, vomit, and then convulse. Heart and lungs then cease to function. The entrance to the factory was hidden behind a statue of Shiva, the Hindu god of destruction.

Asahara announced that he had plans to build "astral hospitals" and spaceships that would deliver himself and his followers to a so-called new civilization he called Shambhala, the name of an idyllic mythical kingdom in Tibetan Buddhism. Here, Asahara and his loyal followers would thrive following the apocalypse.

On a warm summer night in 1994, the cult released sarin into the picturesque city of Matsumoto in an attempt to kill three judges set to rule on a lawsuit brought against the cult. The lawsuit had been filed by a landowner who claimed Aum Shinrikyo had bought land from him by devious means. The landowner said that he wouldn't have sold the property if he had known he was selling it to the cult; the judges were expected to side with the landowner. In addition, the citizens of Matsumoto had angered Aum Shinrikyo when 140,000 locals (almost 70 percent of the city's population) signed a petition against the cult setting up an office and factory on the south side of the city. On June 27, 1994, the cult used a refrigerator truck to release sarin on the very street in Matsumoto where the dorm housing the three judges was located. The truck had been converted into a mobile gas chamber consisting of a heating contraption designed to turn liquid sarin into gas. A gust of wind dispersed the gas, killing seven and injuring hundreds more. An eighth victim—Sumiko Kono—remained in a coma for 14 years after the attack before dying of respiratory failure.

It would later be discovered that the Matsumoto attack was a trial run to test the efficiency of a system that could deliver the deadly gas. Unfortunately, the authorities did not link the attack to the cult—although there were some suspicions—and Aum Shinrikyo continued to prepare assiduously for Armageddon.

On a bright spring morning on March 20, 1995, commuters on their way to work during rush hour stumbled from subway trains on five different lines, all of which converged at Tokyo's Kasumigaseki station. They were clutching their chests, gasping for air, and retching. Some were coughing up blood, while others had been rendered partially blind. One subway worker noticed spilled liquid on the floor and went to mop it up. Moments later, he staggered and fell down dead. Shortly before these terrifying events, five members of Aum Shinrikyo had entered the Tokyo subway system. They were wearing surgical masks and carrying liquid sarin in plastic bags. The cult members were also carrying umbrellas with sharpened tips, which they used to puncture the plastic bags and release the deadly chemical onto floors or in luggage racks. They then exited the trains and made their getaway. Thankfully, the sarin used in the attacks was only 25 percent pure, and most of it remained in liquid rather than gas form.[2] Nevertheless, 13 people died and some 5,500 were injured, many suffering severe vision problems.

After the attack, Asahara went into hiding while his followers denied any involvement. They claimed that the media was trying to undermine the group by linking them to the attack and alleged that Aum Shinrikyo was a victim of police aggression and government oppression. The Great Hanshin earthquake that had hit Kobe, Japan, earlier in the year, killing up to 6,434 people, was portrayed by Shoko Asahara as the fulfillment of a prophecy. In radio broadcasts, Aum Shinrikyo claimed that it was caused by a secret "earthquake machine" owned by the US.

Cult members were so wrapped up in their leader's apocalyptic forebodings that they were unable to acknowledge the terror they had inflicted on their own country. They continued to hand out flyers outside their headquarters in Tokyo, one of which read, "Only members of the Aum will survive Armageddon. Japan is already being attacked by outside forces. You must devote yourself to Master Asahara; he is the only one who can save you." Police suspicions that Aum Shinrikyo were involved in both sarin attacks quickly gained credence when traces of the chemical were found in the soil at their compound. As a result, police planned raids on the cult's Kamikuishiki HQ and on several other Aum Shinrikyo properties throughout Japan.

The raid and Asahara's arrest were broadcast live on television. Amid the heavy morning mist, a squad of riot police clad in armor and wearing protective masks invaded the cult's HQ at the base of Mount Fuji. Hundreds of reporters and journalists gathered at the scene to document the climax of the nation's largest criminal investigation. Regular programming was cancelled for most of the day, and the spectacle would remain etched in the collective memory for years to come.

Once inside the compound, police found Asahara hidden in a coffinlike, fortified room. Rumors had circulated that his arrest might trigger mass suicide among his followers or some other form of retaliatory attack, but there was no resistance and Aum members followed police orders. Police found a number of sect members wandering around aimlessly, malnourished, and smeared with dirt. They also found 53 children wearing distinctive Aum Shinrikyo helmets with wires dangling down from inside; the helmets were supposed to align the wearer's brainwaves with Asahara's. Children living in the cult were sleep deprived and too terrified to go outside because they believed the US military was going to drop bombs of poison on them. Paramedics carried out at least 50 sect members who were too weak, dazed, or ill to walk unaided. Some claimed that they were fasting voluntarily; six were hospitalized for dehydration and malnutrition. Following the raid on the compound, a spokesperson for the cult claimed that the reason they possessed such huge quantities of chemicals was "to fertilize the soil" when Armageddon occurred.[4]

The police operation revealed the alarming extent of Aum Shinrikyo's activities and plans. Police discovered that the cult had been experimenting with biological agents and had even made overtures to the Soviet Union for nuclear weapons and tanks. During questioning, Aum Shinrikyo member Tomomasa Nakagawa confessed that he, along with five other cult members, abducted and murdered the Sakamoto family. He claimed they were ordered to kill the young family and bury their bodies in the mountains of northern Japan. Shortly afterward, police were directed to the burial sites and found the bodies.

Aum members also told police that deserters from the cult were often murdered. In 1989, Shuji Taguchi was strangled to death in a so-called "mercy killing" after he attempted to leave.[3] In 1994, Asahara ordered that Kotaro Ochido, a pharmacist in Aum Shinrikyo, be strangled for attempting to flee the compound. In 1995, Kiyoshi Kariya died during a kidnapping and interrogation session perpetrated by Aum Shinrikyo after he resisted the cult's attempts to persuade his sister to sign over her fortune to it. Other survivors reported that opponents of Aum Shinrikyo would be wiretapped and then murdered.

Across Japan, millions of people followed the disturbing story of the doomsday cult and the ensuing trial. In Hibiya Park, more than 15,000 people lined up to compete in a lottery to win one of the 48 courtroom seats allocated to the public. The prosecutors, who referred to Asahara as "the most vicious criminal in this country's history," argued that he was the mastermind behind the attacks and several other murders.[4] Asahara seemed indifferent to the proceedings, causing anger among the family members of his victims; he either remained silent, giggled, or uttered incomprehensible words. The man who portrayed himself as a messiah now appeared to be anything but, and his counsel claimed he was mentally unfit to stand trial. In a bid to get Shoko Asahara to speak, his lawyers pushed for visits with his daughters, hoping it would bring him out of his shell. However, during these visits, he just grinned and mumbled. On a later occasion, he masturbated in front of one of his daughters. During his trial, Shoko Asahara's defense lawyers attempted to argue that senior followers had initiated the attacks and that Asahara himself was unaware of them. Aum Shinrikyo members contradicted this, however, testifying that Asahara had told the members who perpetrated the attacks that they were redeeming the souls of their victims by killing them.

The case against Asahara was confirmed by confessions from key cult members, and he was found guilty for his role in 13 crimes resulting in the deaths of 29 people, including the Tokyo subway attack; the Matsumoto attack; and the murders of Tsutsumi Sakamoto, his wife, and their baby son. Asahara was sentenced to death by the Tokyo District Court in February 2004. The death penalties meted out to Asahara and his followers were criticized by human rights organization Amnesty International. "Justice demands accountability but also respect for everyone's human rights. The death penalty can never deliver this as it is the ultimate denial of human rights," wrote Hiroka Shoji, East Asia researcher at Amnesty International.[5]

Following an appeal, the sentence was upheld by the Supreme Court, which declared Asahara legally sane and responsible for his actions. In addition to Asahara, 191 Aum Shinrikyo members were indicted for a number of criminal acts. Twelve were also sentenced to death. During a 1991 hearing, cult member Tomomasa Nakagawa, a former doctor who had helped produce the sarin, took the stand and pleaded with Asahara to explain what he was thinking when he ordered his followers to commit violence. "I didn't enter the priesthood [of Aum Shinrikyo] to produce sarin or choke someone's neck. Please explain your ideas to the people who believed in you," Nakagawa begged. Asahara just closed his eyes and mumbled incomprehensibly.[6]

On Friday, July 6, 2018, Shoko Asahara and six other members of the cult—Tomomasa Nakagawa, Tomomitsu Niimi, Kiyohide Hayakawa, Yoshihiro Inoue, Seiichi Endo, and Masami Tsuchiya—were executed by hanging. Twenty days later, another six members of the cult were executed: Satoru Hashimoto, Yasuo Koike Kenichi Hirose, Kazuaki Okazaki, Toru Toyoda, and Masato Yokoyama. The hangings left a number of unexplained questions—in particular, how did the cult attract such brilliant young minds and brainwash them to commit such appalling acts? According to Shoko Egawa, the answer lay in the cult's clever fusion of religion, science, and cyberspace, matters that continue to preoccupy Japanese youth.

In 2000, Aum Shinrikyo made a reappearance. The group had distanced itself from Shoko Asahara and his methods and rebranded itself "Aleph." Apologies were made for the Tokyo metro attacks and compensation paid to victims. In 2007, another splinter group was formed named Kihari no Wa. Almost 2,000 people still follow the rituals of these splinter groups, which are monitored by the Japanese authorities.

---

[1] *San Francisco Chronicle*, May 16, 1995—"Asahara's Strange Path to Notoriety"

[2] *The Atlanta Constitution*, November 5, 1995—"Focus on a Doomsday Cult"

[3] *Japan Times*, July 6, 2018—"Profiles of Top Aum Shinrikyo Members"

[4] *The Town Talk*, April 25, 2003—"Japanese Prosecutors Seeking Death Penalty for Shoko Asahara"

[5] https://www.japantimes.co.jp/news/2018/07/06/national/crime-legal/aum-founders-execution-paves-way-debate-japan-death-penalty/#.XKYqbC-ZMQk

[6] *Japan Times*, July 6, 2018—"Aum Shinrikyo Guru Shoko Ashahara and Six Other Cult Members Hanged for Mass Murders"

Heaven's Gate

The arrival of a comet in the night sky is normally greeted with excitement and a sense of awe. However, for the members of the Heaven's Gate cult, the coming of Hale-Bopp was the signal for them to exit their human "shells" in ritual suicide.

"They could see that even prior to the jail incident, their stability and credibility was by now unquestionably questionable."

Marshall Applewhite

On March 26, 1997, the hills of Rancho Santa Fe, California, where eucalyptus trees line streets of lavish homes, became the scene of a UFO cult's final act. In a sprawling mansion whose walls were adorned with images of extraterrestrials, Marshall Applewhite instructed 38 devoted followers to drink a concoction of alcohol and barbiturates, place bags over their heads, and lie down and die. They believed that they would ascend to a better world via a spaceship that was traveling to Earth in the wake of the Hale-Bopp comet.

Marshall Applewhite grew up in a nomadic but close-knit family. His father, Marshall Applewhite Sr., was a well-known Presbyterian minister who moved his family around southern Texas, founding and building churches. The family eventually settled in Corpus Christi, where, in 1948, Applewhite graduated high school. He majored in philosophy at Austin College and was remembered as having a strong, extrovert personality and talent as a singer—he sang 15 roles with the Houston Grand Opera. He subsequently enrolled at the Union Theological Seminary of Virginia. At this period, there was no indication of the zealot that Applewhite would ultimately become. He was interested in following in his father's footsteps, and a career in music also held attractions for him. Eventually, Applewhite dropped out and took a job as a music director at a Presbyterian church near Charlotte, North Carolina. Around this time, Applewhite married a fellow Texan, Anne Pearce. The marriage resulted in two children, but eventually ended in divorce for reasons unknown.

In 1954, Applewhite was drafted into the army, serving in Salzburg, Austria, and White Sands, New Mexico. Following his honorable discharge in 1956, Applewhite studied music at the University of Colorado, earning a master's degree, and starred in a number of the school's musical productions, including *Oklahoma* and *South Pacific*. After graduating, Applewhite headed back to Texas and took a post as a music professor at the University of St. Thomas, a private Catholic college in downtown Houston. However, Applewhite was subsequently fired, allegedly for having an affair with one of his male students. According to a report in *The Houston Chronicle*, he was let go for "health problems of an emotional nature."

Throughout the late 1960s, Applewhite was obsessed with the space race and the moon landing in 1969 in particular. He saw this "giant leap for mankind" as a groundbreaking moment in history and as his opportunity to launch his own spiritual voyage. "The act of landing on the moon was an epiphany," said Brad Steiger, author of *Inside Heaven's Gate*. "[It] opened up the door to everything . . ."

Applewhite's voyage into the bizarre truly began in 1972, when he was hospitalized in Houston following a mental breakdown. By this point, he was estranged from his wife and two children and had experienced a number of unsatisfactory homosexual relationships. He had told friends that he was considering giving up relationships for good, but that he also yearned for a companion. In this Houston hospital, Applewhite's life changed forever when he met Bonnie Nettles, a 44-year-old married mother of four, who was working as a nurse. Nettles had a keen interest in the occult and astrology and offered to create an astrological chart for him. She convinced Applewhite that he "had a purpose" and "that God had kept him alive" for a special reason.[1] The unlikely duo became platonic friends, bonding over their shared interests in astrology, mysticism, and New Age ideologies. For a brief period, they opened a Houston bookstore together that focused on astrology, theosophy, and metaphysics.

One day, while camping on the Oregon coast, they came to the conclusion that they were the two witnesses described in the Book of Revelation, destined to be martyred and resurrected before a disbelieving world.[2] Nettles quit her job and abandoned her family to join Applewhite on their joint spiritual journey. Applewhite and Nettles—once devout Christians—came to believe that they were aliens from the "Next Level" sent to Earth to recruit humans to join them when they returned to outer space. Preaching about a new life in outer space quickly won them attention and notoriety. For over two decades, they were simply known as "The Two." Sometimes they called themselves Bo and Peep or Do and Ti, among other quirky names.

The 1970s was a time for mass spiritual searching; the US had been traumatized by the Vietnam War, as well as years of social upheaval and violence. Many people who wound up in Applewhite and Nettles' group had already tried yoga, astrology, as well as hallucinogenic drugs, but still felt unfulfilled. Listening to "The Two," they believed that they had finally found the spiritual truth they had been searching for.

Apocalyptic millennialism soon became the focus of Applewhite and Nettles' belief system. They spent the next several years recruiting disciples for their new religion—initially called Human Individual Metamorphosis (HIM)—which mixed together apocalyptic Christianity with belief in extraterrestrials and UFOs. Applewhite and Nettles were massive fans of the TV show *Star Trek* and the 1977 movie *Close Encounters of the Third Kind*.

According to Applewhite and Nettles, to be saved from Lucifer and join their nomadic ministry, acolytes had to be willing to give up all earthly pleasures and be ready to leave the planet on an alien spacecraft for a better life. When this spaceship arrived to carry the followers away, their bodies would evolve into an extraterrestrial form. HIM toured across the US, recruiting like-minded people. They created a national stir in Waldport, Oregon, when 20 residents suddenly disappeared following a HIM recruitment meeting. It transpired that they had abandoned families and friends to join HIM in its journey across the country. One such was John M. Craig from Florida, who suddenly walked out on his wife and six children, leaving behind a note that read, "I'm going to Florida to catch a spaceship."[3]

The cult had several brushes with the law when defectors and followers' relatives accused Applewhite and Nettles of theft and brainwashing. The husband of one convert accused them of fraud, stating that they had used his wife's credit card without her knowledge, and "The Two" were subsequently arrested. Charges were dropped after the wife claimed that she knew they were using her credit card; however, the arrest turned up another warrant against Applewhite—for the theft of a rental car. While Applewhite and Nettles were recruiting, they often defaulted on motel and car rental bills; sometimes they didn't even return their rental car. As a result, Applewhite served six months in prison in Missouri.

Following his release, he addressed this experience in the third person, stating, "They could see that even prior to the jail incident, their stability and credibility was by now unquestionably questionable. The felon record was taken in stride as assurance that now they couldn't turn back." Robert Balch, a University of Montana sociologist, infiltrated the cult for two months in 1975. He discovered that adherents were forced to beg for money and abide by strict rules of discipline, including reporting to Applewhite and Nettles at 12-minute intervals throughout the day. Despite the strict regime, in a 1994 interview with the *Chicago Tribune*, Balch was adamant that HIM was not a dangerous cult.

Almost as fast as HIM had entered the limelight, it vanished. In 1976, after a number of disillusioned followers abandoned the group, it went underground, existing in deep seclusion in a number of southwestern cities. HIM returned to public notice once again in 1992 with a brand-new name—Heaven's Gate—and a brand-new computer business named Higher Source that sustained its existence. According to the Heaven's Gate book, which was written by Applewhite, they "were very much 'lifted out' of this world—literally."[4] Nettles had passed away in 1985—or as Applewhite put it, had "separated from her borrowed human container and returned to the Next Level."

Applewhite was now more determined than ever to reach a broader public with his beliefs. Armed with an updated manifesto, he began to create videos urging people to join him. Initially, these broadcasts only lured back Applewhite's "lost sheep"—followers that had previously abandoned the group. Applewhite now maintained that he and his acolytes would ascend to outer space without their human "vehicles," instead transferring their consciousness into aliens that would be waiting for them aboard a spaceship. The body was merely a "temporary container for the soul."[5] In May 1993, Applewhite placed an advert titled "UFO Cult Resurfaces with Final Offer." In the article, which was basically a recruitment advertisement, Applewhite warned that the Earth was about to be recycled and that if anybody wanted to live, they must join Heaven's Gate.

During January 1994, Applewhite and his followers staged public meetings and interviews across the country. By this point, Applewhite's followers had completely abandoned their previous lives and families and embarked on diets to cleanse their bodies, such as the Master Cleanse juice fast invented by Stanley Burroughs in the 1940s. Members also renounced all forms of sexuality, even agreeing to castration. Marshall Applewhite never forced his followers to be castrated. Eight men, including Applewhite, voluntarily went under the knife. Applewhite believed "The Next Level" was a place without gender and he wanted to ensure he remained celibate.

Applewhite decreed that total familial separation was necessary because Earth's human structures were being controlled by demonic forces. People abandoned spouses and children to follow Heaven's Gate, whose doctrine was now a blend of evangelical Christianity and New Age science fiction.

Heaven's Gate mostly consisted of middle-aged men and women with enough intelligence to run a booming computer business to sustain their way of life. In 1995, Applewhite took his message to the internet, publishing statements with titles such as "Undercover 'Jesus' Surfaces Before Departure." His posts were met with "ridicule, hostility, or both." According to his book, negative responses were an indication that the "weeds" of humanity had taken over the Earth's "garden" and were the signal for him to begin his preparations to return "home." In October 1996, Applewhite published two videos dedicated to warning the world of its impending doom. They were titled *Planet About to Be Recycled. Your Only Chance to Survive— Leave with Us* and *Last Chance to Evacuate Earth Before It's Recycled.*

Applewhite saw the coming Hale-Bopp comet as a signal that Heaven's Gate's time had come to finally leave Earth. According to the Heaven's Gate website, Hale-Bopp was the "marker we've been waiting for—the time for the arrival of the spacecraft from the Level Above Human to take us home to 'Their World'—in the literal Heavens." Applewhite was convinced that Hale-Bopp was concealing a spaceship and, as the comet passed over California, he and his followers would ascend onto this spaceship and depart for a better world.

On March 22 and 23, 1997, all 39 active members of Heaven's Gate committed suicide in a rented mansion, 18241 Colina Norte, in the San Diego suburb of Rancho Santa Fe. The number 39 had special significance for Marshall Applewhite because 3 plus 9 equals 12—the number of Christ's disciples. These long-time devotees consisted of 21 women and 18 men, ranging in age from 26 to 72. They included computer experts, musicians, teachers, fathers, and grandmothers. Before the final act, they had a celebratory last meal in Marie Callender's, a local restaurant where they rented out the banquet room. For their final dinner, the cult members all ate the same meal: salad with tomato vinegar dressing, turkey pot pie, followed by blueberry cheesecake.

Once back at the mansion, the cult filmed themselves making emotional statements about their beliefs and saying their final goodbyes. They expressed gratitude that they had been given the opportunity to escape impending Armageddon and shed their "containers" to go to the "Level Above Human." They detailed what Heaven's Gate meant to them and explained why they had to end their terrestrial lives. They also updated the Heaven's Gate website with the message, "Hale-Bopp brings closure to Heaven's Gate . . . Our 22 years of classroom here on planet Earth are finally coming to conclusion—'graduation' from the Human Evolutionary Level. We are happily prepared to leave 'this world' and go with Ti's crew."

While sky-watchers in the West were enjoying a lunar eclipse, Applewhite and 38 of his followers were making preparations for their interstellar journey. They packed travel kits and stuffed their pockets with $5 bills and quarters to avoid being stranded anywhere without money for transportation. They donned black tracksuits with "Heaven's Gate Away Team" patches embroidered on the front—a homage to the *Star Trek* concept of temporary visitors to planets—and black Nike sneakers. They then ingested a toxic mixture of barbiturates with applesauce, chased down with a shot of vodka. They tied plastic bags around their heads and lay down on their beds to await death. This procedure was carried out in three waves. When the first group died, the second group shrouded them in purple sheets. This was possibly an echo of ancient burial customs with the color purple symbolizing Easter and also to commemorate Nettles, whose favorite color was purple. The final two men were responsible for meticulously cleaning the house and then killing themselves.

Police were alerted to the mass suicides when cult member Rio DiAngelo returned to the rented mansion to find the tragic death scene. He had left the cult the previous month and had decided to visit the house after receiving a videotape from the group. In 2007, he wrote a book about his experiences with Heaven's Gate titled *Beyond Human Mind: The Soul Evolution of Heaven's Gate*.

Two months after the mass suicides, cult members Wayne Cooke and Charles Humphrey attempted to commit suicide with barbiturates in a hotel room a few miles from the Rancho Santa Fe mansion. Cooke succeeded in ending his life, but Humphrey failed. Cooke publicly stated that he regretted not going to the "mother craft" with his wife, who had committed suicide with the cult. Cooke and his wife left behind a 10-year-old daughter.

In February 1998, Humphrey killed himself with carbon monoxide in a tent in the Arizona desert near Ehrenberg. Like the others, he was wearing a "Heaven's Gate Away Team" patch on his t-shirt and had a $5 bill and coins in his pocket. Beside his body was a note reading "Do Not Revive."

The cult's mass suicide spawned a number of cruel jokes. "Just Did It" quipped one website, parodying the famous Nike trademark "Just do it." The TV show *Saturday Night Live* also based a skit on the incident.

Heaven's Gate has the dubious distinction of being the first infamous American cult of the internet era. It was the brainchild of a sexually troubled musician turned cult leader, who recruited susceptible people who felt alienated from a corrupt and, to them, doomed world. Snaps of the tragic crime scene—the Nike sneakers, the black tracksuits, the purple shrouds—were seared into the public consciousness. In death, Marshall Applewhite finally left the planet from which he had spent two decades dreaming of escaping, leaving behind the largest mass suicide on US soil. In the aftermath, many dismissed the followers of Heaven's Gate as deluded fantasists, but in reality, their beliefs—albeit extreme—did not differ too much from those of mainstream religions: a belief in a higher power, a belief in the importance of soul over body, and a belief in the eternal fight of good against evil. The website heavensgate.com is still active. The site outlines the cult's belief system, as well as the "exit videos" they recorded before committing suicide.

———————————

[1] *The Atlanta Constitution*, March 29, 1997—"The Two: Pied Pipers who led the way to Death"
[2] *Heaven's Gate: America's UFO Religion* by Benjamin E. Zeller
[3] *Chicago Sun-Times*, March 30, 1997—"Cult Leader's Son Offers Apology to Members' Kin"
[4] *The Vancouver Sun*, March 29, 1997—"Cult Message of an Afterlife in Space Met with Derision"
[5] *The New York Times*, March 28, 1997—"On the Furthest Fringes of Millennialism"

Movement for the Restoration of the Ten Commandments of God

A blazing, boarded-up church and mass graves became final resting places for hundreds of devotees of the Movement for the Restoration of the Ten Commandments of God. They suffered agonizing deaths for their leaders' greed and ruthless, murderous manipulations.

"I've been receiving messages from God
that the Virgin Mary is annoyed.
People are sinning too much and God
is going to end the world because of the sins."

Credonia Mwerinde

On March 17, 2000, the world awoke to the grim news that hundreds of followers of the Movement for the Restoration of Ten Commandments of God had burned to death inside their compound in the mist-shrouded Kanungu district of southwestern Uganda. Pictures soon started to emerge of a cult ravaged by greed; gullibility; and, when the cult leaders' prophecy of an apocalypse didn't transpire, appalling violence.

The Movement for the Restoration of the Ten Commandments of God was a breakaway religious movement from the Roman Catholic Church. It was founded in Uganda in the late 1980s by Credonia Mwerinde and Joseph Kibweteere. Mwerinde claimed she had spiritual powers and had witnessed apparitions of the Virgin Mary, while Kibweteere was a pillar of the local community. Thanks to a chance encounter, they came together to form one of the deadliest cults in history.

A wealthy farmer and former school administrator, Kibweteere was a prominent member of the Roman Catholic Democratic Party in the 1960s and 1970s. He established a Catholic church near his home after being inspired to do so by a pilgrimage to Rome in 1975. He was devoted to the church, attending mass every single day. However, his political career ended in 1980, when the rival Ugandan People's Congress won the general election. Kibweteere had 16 children by four different women. His wife Theresa raised all the children as her own on their farm near Kambuga.

In stark contrast, Mwerinde sold banana beer and bootleg liquor at a local village market in Manungu, approximately 20 miles (32 km) away. She was promiscuous and rumored to be a prostitute.[1] In 1988, Mwerinde claimed that, during a vision, the Virgin Mary warned that those who did not strictly adhere to the Ten Commandments would suffer apocalyptic damnation. She subsequently called herself a high priestess and held local meetings about her visions. At one of these meetings the following year, she met Kibweteere. During her speech, Mwerinde announced to the audience that she had had a vision to find a man named "Kibweteere" who would help her spread her message about the coming apocalypse.

Shortly afterward, Mwerinde, her two children, her sister, and her niece moved in with Kibweteere and his deeply religious family. "At first, I believed what she was saying," said Kibweteere's wife, Theresa.[2] However, Mwerinde soon took control of the household, ordering everybody to sleep on mats while she took the master bedroom. She told Kibweteere that he would become the leader of their new religious movement to be named the Restoration of the Ten Commandments of God. He already had a sizable following within the local Catholic community and was the perfect figurehead in a country where male leadership was deemed necessary for legitimacy and success. Before long, Kibweteere was claiming to experience visions as well. At first, the cult's message was simple: adhere to the Ten Commandments. Because of this, the duo successfully manipulated religious leaders into believing that Mwerinde was the embodiment of the Virgin Mary's foreboding message. They recruited four Catholic priests—John Kamagara, Dominic Kataribabo, Joseph Kasapurari, and Paul Ikazire—who, along with Mwerinde and Kibweteere, became leaders of the cult. They also created a 163-page handbook titled *A Timely Message from Heaven: The End of Present Times,* which they distributed across Uganda and Rwanda.[3] It offered an alluring message of salvation to African villagers struggling with poverty and disease. Unbelievers were offered a very different fate: an eternity in hell. Over the forthcoming years, The Movement for the Restoration of the Ten Commandments of God recruited around 5,000 followers, mostly disaffected Roman Catholics.

The cult quickly earned a controversial reputation for its strict rules and bizarre behavior. When new members joined, they were required to fill out a questionnaire about whether they would be willing to die for their faith.[4] Followers were forbidden to have sex or use soap and were forced to kneel and pray for hours on the church's concrete floor. They were ordered to wear green robes and forbidden to speak except to utter prayers or sing hymns. To communicate, they had to use sign language. They were frequently required to fast and to work long hours in the fields under the blistering sun. Mwerinde and the other cult leaders secured followers' unwavering loyalty by invoking visions that they claimed came from the Virgin Mary. Meanwhile, Mwerinde's domination of the Kibweteere household had revealed a penchant for extreme cruelty. She exploded in rage and beat anybody who questioned her authority or refused to do her bidding. By this point, around 200 other followers had moved into Kibweteere's home, and Mwerinde had banished his children to a 15 by 40 ft (4.6 by 12 m) shed in the backyard. The shed's windows were nailed shut, and the children were forced to sleep on a dirty floor; many contracted the contagious skin disease scabies.

The cult's leaders separated mothers and fathers from their children. They also stopped children from going to school, supposedly in order to keep them free from sin and ensure that they would go to heaven. "These days . . . the majority of youths go to hell; only very few go to heaven in a day," read the cult's handbook.[5]

Despite the warning signs of her mental instability, the cult's devotees remained convinced that Mwerinde was a prophet. She soon revealed another prophecy: that the world was going to end in 1992. When 1992 came and the apocalypse failed to materialize, Mwerinde announced that God had been kind enough to grant more time for repentance, and life in the cult resumed. However, following the failed apocalypse, the leaders tightened their grip over their acolytes, violating their basic human rights to an education and to freedom. They completely cut their followers off from society and took advantage of the AIDS epidemic that, since the early 1980s, had claimed the lives of hundreds of thousands of Ugandans by claiming that the disease was God's punishment for sinners. Punishments were meted out to doubters. "I've been receiving messages from God that the Virgin Mary is annoyed," Mwerinde declared. "People are sinning too much and God is going to end the world because of the sins."[6] The cult leaders forbade alcohol, claiming that alcohol was controlled by Satan, as were witch doctors and cats and dogs. "From these animals, Satan is actually fighting against man, particularly those who own animals," read the cult's updated handbook.

Around this time, the local bishop threatened that members would be excommunicated from the Catholic Church, and Paul Ikazire decided to leave the cult. He wasn't the only one becoming disillusioned, and eventually Kibweteere's family urged him to expel Mwerinde from their home. When he refused, they forced her out, and Kibweteere went with her. The cult subsequently moved to Mwerinde's farm, located just outside Kanungu. As their wealth increased, they built 12 more buildings there, turning it into a sprawling commune for their still-growing cult.

Following this relocation, Mwerinde once again predicted that the world was going to end—this time on December 31, 1999. She preached that massive snakes and large blocks of cement would fall from heaven onto sinners and that there would be three days of consecutive darkness that would engulf the entire world. However, according to Mwerinde, the Movement for the Restoration of the Ten Commandments of God would survive thanks to their faith: Their compound had been chosen as the new Israel. "The Lord told me that hurricanes of fire would rain forth from heaven and spread over those who would not have repented . . . This fire will also reach inside the buildings; there is no way one can escape."[6]

To prepare for doomsday, Mwerinde ordered cult members to sell their homes and donate the proceeds to the cult. When the world ended, they would no longer need possessions, as the Earth would belong to them and they would be able to communicate directly with Jesus.

On New Year's Eve 1999, the cult began the countdown for the end of the world. Unsurprisingly, the world did not end with the dawn of the new millennium. Faced by a group of disillusioned and impoverished followers, some of whom were demanding their money back, the cult leaders devised a cruel plan. In early March, they ordered members to pray, fast, and clean the compound to prepare for the arrival of some special visitors.

The cult held a massive party at the compound in Kanungu on

March 16, 2000. Three bulls were roasted and 70 crates of Coca-Cola drunk. The following morning, hundreds of cult members were herded into the compound's mud-brick church, named the Ark, a reference to Noah's ark in the Bible. Once everyone was inside, the windows and doors were boarded up and nailed shut and the church was doused with gasoline. At around 11 a.m., the building erupted in flames. As local people were quietly getting on with their lives in the lush mountainous area of Kanungu, they suddenly saw clouds of smoke billowing from the cult's compound. Rushing to the scene, they heard terrified screams coming from inside the burning church. By the time the police arrived, it was already too late: Everyone inside the church was dead. "So many burned beyond recognition," recalled Corporal Stephen Mujuni. "We got there when the fire was still on. You could see some people's scars glowing with fire, red hot fire."[7]

It was initially thought that the cult's leaders had died in the fire with their followers in a mass suicide. However, a couple of days later, while local authorities were searching the cult's compound, they came across six bodies stuffed into a latrine pit—the first indication that cult members may have not died willingly. Several mass graves were then discovered around Kanungu: 153 bodies were unearthed at Buhunga, where new members were indoctrinated; 155 bodies were unearthed at Dominic Kataribabo's estate in Rugazi, where members attended courses in dormitories; 81 bodies were unearthed in Rushojwa; and another 55 were unearthed in Buziga, an upscale, residential suburb of Kampala. Children and babies made up a large portion of the bodies uncovered in the mass graves. The exhumed bodies showed evidence of poisoning. There was also evidence that many had been strangled or beaten to death. "The people who sold their property would inquire one by one," said 17-year-old cult member Peter Ahimbisibwe. "Whoever would inquire would disappear."[8] One of the few cult members to survive, Peter was not present at the cult's compound on that fateful morning, as he had slipped away to find some food.[9] His mother, Noel Gorret, and his sister, Fortunate, both perished in the church fire.

When it became apparent that all the evidence pointed to mass murder rather than mass suicide, Buganda Road Court issued an international warrant for the arrest of the cult leaders. However, they were nowhere to be found. During the final weeks in the compound, they had sold the most valuable property, and there was speculation that they had absconded with the proceeds. Police discovered that, in the days leading up to the mass murder, cult leader Dominic Kataribabo had traveled to the town of Kasese to purchase a large supply of sulfuric acid—presumably to accelerate the fire. However, aside from this information, the investigation was plagued with problems. Local police were undertrained and under-resourced and ultimately, they couldn't even determine which cult leaders, if any, had survived the inferno. They were also unable to determine how many people had died in the fire or fully identify those who had. At first, it was reported that 530 people had died, then that figure was revised down to around 330. Other researchers claimed that as many as 1,000 people could have perished. Today, it is widely accepted that Credonia Mwerinde and Joseph Kibweteere both survived. In 2014, Kibweteere was rumored to be hiding somewhere in Malawi but, according to his wife, he died in July 1999 after a long "mental illness" and his body was buried in a garden at Rugazi in southwestern Uganda.[10]

The Ugandan authorities' failure to fully investigate so many deaths or to track down any of the cult leaders caused national and international concern. To this day, there has not been a single arrest or even a trial in absentia. As a result, full details of the cult's murderous actions remain unknown and will likely remain so.

———————

[1] *The Des Moines Register*, April 2, 2000—"Signs of Cult Massacre Went Unheeded"

[2] *The Missoulian*, April 2, 2000—"Inside Uganda's Doomsday Cult"

[3] *San Antonio Express-News*, April 5, 2000—"Uganda's Sect Handbook Offers Stark Vision"

[4] *The New York Times*, April 2, 2000—"Uganda Cult's Mystique Finally Turned Deadly"

[5] *St. Louis Post-Dispatch*, April 3, 2000—"Followers of Movement Believed Childhood Was an Occasion of Sin"

[6] *The Seattle Times*, March 31, 2000—"Kibwetere's Wife Says He Did Not Run Uganda Cult"

[7] *Ghosts of Kanungu* by Richard Vokes

[8] *The Daytona Beach News-Journal*, April 3, 2000—"Ugandans Gather to Mourn 924 Victims of Doomsday Cult"

[9] *Akron Beacon Journal*, April 2, 2000—"Many In Uganda Missed Warning Signs About Cult"

[10] BBC Monitoring International Reports, May 20, 2011—"Cult Leader Linked to Mass Murder in Southwest Is Dead, Wife Says"

NXIVM

For almost two decades, NXIVM promoted itself as a successful, dedicated self-help organization. In reality, the world of NXIVM was one of sex slavery, extortion, and child abuse. At its center was a secretive, self-proclaimed guru named Keith Raniere.

———————————

"I believed Keith Raniere's intentions were

to help people, and I was wrong."

Allison Mack

———————————

NXIVM (pronounced Nexium) was founded in 1998 by Keith Raniere and Nancy Salzman in Clifton Park, Albany, New York. Raniere claimed he chose Salzman as his business partner after interviewing hundreds of people. She was, in effect, his first follower. In NXIVM, Raniere was known as "Vanguard." Salzman, a former psychiatric nurse, was "Prefect."

Also known as Executive Success Programs Inc., NXIVM was a company offering self-help workshops focused on business improvement and radical self-empowerment. Four years earlier, Raniere's multimillion-dollar discount buying club, Consumers' Buyline, had collapsed after investigations by 23 states and two federal agencies alleged it was a pyramid scheme. In 1997, Raniere paid a fine of $40,000 and agreed to a ban from future involvement in any chain-distribution scheme. NXIVM would also prove to be a pyramid scheme, but of a different kind.

NXIVM was supposedly designed to bring about greater self-fulfillment by eliminating psychological barriers through a process it termed "rational inquiry." This often involved tracing members' fears or phobias back to childhood incidents. Raniere promised that, with his help, people could conquer long-held fears and insecurities and overcome mindsets that had held them back and led them to become victimized. Once past worries and fears had been worked through, the "unified" Nxian could go on to joyfully achieve their life goals. Journalist and author Vanessa Grigoriadis, granted rare, if, by her own admission, "stage-managed" access to this most secretive of groups, wrote in the *New York Times Magazine*, May 30, 2018: "The ultimate NXIVM member was . . . not only rich but emotionally disciplined, self-controlled, attractive, physically fit, and slender—or, using the term that most members themselves preferred, 'badass.'"

This self-enlightenment came with a hefty price tag. NXIVM's Ethos program could be purchased, just like a health club membership, for $1,800 a year. Hundreds of modules were offered with titles such as "Work and Value" and "Best People; Perfect World." NXIVM also offered "intensives" of 16 days that cost $7,500. During these, people worked from 8 a.m to 9 p.m.[1] NXIVM students had to sign strict nondisclosure agreements forbidding them to share material or information from the program.

Students who achieved success on NXIVM courses were given a rank that was indicated by sashes of various colors, much like belts in martial arts. After two years, a member might be promoted from a white sash to a yellow sash and trained to become an unpaid coach for NXIVM. As a coach, a member was expected to bring new recruits into the organization, for which they would receive commission. One member who had worked her way to the top was actress Allison Mack, best known for her role as Clark Kent's friend Chloe Sullivan in the TV series *Smallville*.

NXIVM particularly appealed to wealthy and insecure women who were looking for spiritual and physical betterment. Raniere touted himself as a great intellect with one of the highest IQs in the world; members bowed when "Vanguard" entered the room. NXIVM teachers—who were mostly women—claimed that Raniere was "like a Buddhist monk, living beyond the list of the senses." Raniere told his followers that he had achieved the highest state of human consciousness; accordingly, he was the only member who sported a black sash.

NXIVM grew to over 16,000 members in chapters nationwide, as well as in Canada and Mexico. While initially hailed as a success, somewhere along the line, NXIVM took a dark turn. Controversies soon began to emerge, and news outlets—including *Forbes, Vanity Fair,* and the *New York Post*—started to run disturbing articles about the organization. In response, NXIVM was extremely combative, filing lawsuits against former members and also journalists.

A number of people with connections to NXIVM filed complaints with law-enforcement agencies, alleging that NXIVM was a cult and that they had been brainwashed and abused in various ways. NXIVM held "EMs," (Explorations of Meaning), one-on-one question-and-answer sessions, during which a high-ranking member would probe lower-ranking members' fears and childhood traumas for misperceptions that had made certain memories painful. EMs were supposed to help less-advanced members deal with inner conflict. However, these sessions were also a tool to gain deep personal knowledge of a person in order to use it against them later. "What he kind of does is, he elicits as much information as he can, almost as a friend you're sharing with," said Toni Natalie, an ex-girlfriend of Raniere. "Then he takes those things and he manipulates you with them."

Math teacher Nellie Forst paid for a five-day seminar at NXIVM, hoping for enlightenment and career advice. However, after just one day, she left and demanded her money back. "I consider the 11 hours

I spent at the place to be psychological rape. It left me a totally different person with all this fear I never had before," she said.[2]

Other former members depicted Raniere as a man who manipulated every aspect of NXIVM members' lives. He forced women to have sex with him and ordered them to stick to a strict 500-calorie-a-day diet to achieve the gaunt figure that he found most attractive. There were also a number of allegations from former members that Raniere gained the trust of minors or their Nxian parents and sexually molested them. NXIVM member Heidi Hutchinson once confronted Keith Raniere for allegedly raping her 15-year-old sister Gina, after Hiedi caught him sneaking out of Gina's bedroom window. Gina later went to live in a monastery, and, in October 2002, committed suicide; Heidi blamed Raniere. A 14-year-old girl earlier reported to police that she was raped by Raniere "approximately 60 times" when she was just 12 years old. "I was perfect picking—insecure at the time," she later recalled.[3] Police asked the unnamed victim to wear a wire and confront Raniere. When she refused out of fear, they asked her to sign a waiver saying that he had raped her but agreed not to pursue charges.[4]

According to Toni Natalie, Raniere was a sex maniac who forced himself on women involved with NXIVM, including underage girls. She claimed that while she was in a relationship with Raniere, he had raped her numerous times, claiming she needed to "share in his energy."[5] When Natalie broke up with Raniere, he pleaded with her to come back. He wrote a letter laced with threats of imprisonment and death if she did not return. When she ignored him, several NXIVM followers broke into her house and begged her to return. When it became clear that she wasn't going to do so, she was sued numerous times over accusations relating to her health food store.

Another woman to come forward with allegations against NXIVM was Barbara Bouchey, another of Raniere's past lovers. According to Bouchey, Raniere had "borrowed" more than $1.6 million from her and had allegedly lost it in bad investments. When she abandoned NXIVM, Raniere sued her using six different law firms. He accused her of misappropriation of funds and extortion and, eventually, she had to file for bankruptcy. The charges were eventually dismissed, but Bouchey never recovered her money.

Yet another target was Joseph O'Hara, a former NXIVM consultant. O'Hara had quit when he discovered that Raniere was involved in tax evasion and had been hiring private detectives to spy on people he perceived as enemies. O'Hara had to file for bankruptcy after Raniere launched a series of lawsuits against him.[6]

Despite the controversy and criticism, NXIVM continued to grow, funneling millions of dollars from the hopeful and wealthy. But in 2017, this international "self-help" organization was rocked by fresh allegations. Scores of members claimed that Raniere had created a secretive group within NXIVM. Women claimed they had been coerced into joining a slave-master club and branded with a logo that combined the initials of Keith Raniere and Allison Mack. This master-slave club was known as Dominus Obsequious Sororium (D.O.S.), which translates as "Master Over the Obedient Female Companions." The women involved in this so-called sorority were lured by "Master" Mack on a promise of female empowerment. They were ordered to provide "collateral" in order to join. This consisted of information or material that the prospective "slave" would not want publicly released because it would ruin their reputation or upset someone close to them. They were told that this was protocol to prevent them from divulging the workings of the group to outsiders. However, in reality, this collateral was used as blackmail to force women into having sexual relations with Raniere. Some women handed over sexually explicit photographs of themselves, while others told damaging stories about their personal lives, friends, or family. Once indoctrinated, these women were forced to undertake free, effectively slave labor, as well as engage in sexual services for Raniere.

The lid was finally blown off the cult's nefarious practices when former member and actress Sarah Edmondson and several other women divulged information to *The New York Times* about the secret sorority. The newspaper subsequently ran an exposé detailing torture and sexual exploitation. Edmondson told the newspaper that she was only informed about the secret sorority after giving up collateral in the form of a letter detailing past indiscretions. Edmondson said that, shortly thereafter, she and several other women were invited to an initiation ceremony in Clifton Park. They were blindfolded and taken to a condo, where they were stripped naked. Next, they were held down on a massage table by Nancy Salzman, who instructed them to say, "Master, please brand me, it would be an honor." The women were then branded with a cauterizing iron in the pubic area. The crude markings were performed by a female doctor associated with the cult. The entire procedure took 20 to 30 minutes, and the smell of burning flesh filled the room. "I went the whole time," recollected Edmondson. "I disassociated out of my body."[7] In response to the *New York Times* piece, Raniere claimed they had hired unnamed "experts" who found no evidence to corroborate the allegations. He confessed that the sex-slave sorority existed but denied he had any involvement in it, adding that his "experts" investigated the sorority and found no evidence of abuse. Initially, the Department of Health declined to investigate. However, after the *New York Times* article, the authorities began to look into the matter.

In addition to the reports about the sex-slave sorority, it was alleged that NXIVM sponsored brain-activity studies and other human behavioral studies. These included "fright studies," which consisted of showing adherents graphic videos depicting gang rapes and beheadings and recording their reactions. It was also alleged that Raniere had kept slaves in his home, mostly undocumented immigrants who he threatened with deportation.

Other members of NXIVM were also accused of crimes. Two of NXIVM's most prominent members were Clare and Sara Bronfman, daughters of the late billionaire Edgar Bronfman, chairman of Canadian conglomerate Seagram. Before Edgar Bronfman's death in 2013, he hadn't spoken to his daughters in years because of the millions of dollars they had donated to NXIVM. "I think it's a cult," he said to *Forbes* in 2003. The Bronfman sisters were alleged to have hired various investigative firms and paid them to illegally obtain personal and financial records of six federal judges, as well as journalists and others they perceived to be enemies of NXIVM. It was reported that Clare Bronfman had planted a key logger virus on her father's computer so that NXIVM could monitor his emails, including exchanges with Hillary Clinton while she was running for president. Several members of NXIVM, including Nancy Salzman, allegedly hacked into the computer accounts of so-called enemies of NXIVM at the behest of Raniere. It was also suggested that Raniere had taken $65.6 million from the wealthy sisters but "lost" it in commodities trading. However, there were never any records kept of these trades, and the Bronfman sisters could not provide any receipts documenting where the money went. Raniere allegedly also took another $26 million from the sisters for a real estate scam.

When an FBI investigation began in November 2017, Raniere fled to Mexico. A criminal complaint charging Raniere with multiple counts of sex trafficking and forced labor led, in March 2018, to Raniere's arrest by Mexican police while he was staying in a luxury $10,000-a-week villa outside Puerto Vallarta. Raniere had been difficult to track down; he had been using end-to-end encrypted emails and had stopped using his cell phone.[8] The following month, Allison Mack was indicted on sex trafficking charges. Prosecutors claimed that the sex-slave ring was led by Raniere but that Mack was a co-conspirator, reporting directly to Raniere. Several other people associated with NXIVM were also charged with federal crimes that included sex trafficking, conspiracy to commit forced labor, racketeering, and money laundering. In April 2019, Allison Mack; Nancy Salzman; Lauren Salzman; Clare Bronfman; and NXIVM's bookkeeper, Kathy Russell, pleaded guilty to various charges. After confessing to blackmailing women in the sex-slave sorority to have sex with Keith Raniere, Allison Mack apologized, stating, "I believed Keith Raniere's intentions were to help people, and I was wrong."[9]

Raniere stood trial alone. He faced charges that included racketeering, racketeering conspiracy, human trafficking, sex trafficking, and sexual exploitation of a child. The court heard testimony from a number of women who had been lured into D.O.S. One woman, identified only as "Nicole," said that she joined the sex-slave sorority after she was forced to write a letter to a news outlet falsely accusing her father of sexual assault as collateral. She was later blindfolded and taken to a cabin, where she was tied down on a table. Raniere circled her on the table asking her confrontational questions about her sexual history, while another "slave" performed a sexual act on her.

Another victim, identified only as "Camilla," told the court that Raniere forced women to send him group "crotch shots." Testimony also included a nude photo of an unidentified 15-year-old girl that was found on Raniere's computer and a video of Raniere talking about how the age of sexual consent differs from country to country and from state to state. "Most people scream abuse, and a lot of times the screaming of abuse is abuse in itself. Some little children are perfectly happy with it," he said.[10] The woman in the photograph, who was identified only as Daniela, also testified against Raniere. She said that she and her family left Mexico to join NXIVM and, shortly afterward, Raniere began to sexually abuse her and her underage sisters, one of whom was Camilla.

Text messages from Raniere to Daniela revealed that he expected complete obedience from his so-called slaves. "I need a vow of absolute obedience. I expect you to text me this vow now," read one. In another, Raniere said he wanted Daniela to "find other virgins" for him.[11] Daniela said that Raniere nicknamed her "Norelco" after the shaver because she lacked pubic hair. Later on, Raniere had her confined to a room for two years because she had developed romantic feelings for another man. It was against his rules for any woman he was interested in to be intimate with anybody other than himself.

The trial finished after six weeks of often distressing testimony. Keith Raniere called no witnesses; the only time he spoke publicly was to confirm to the judge that he would not be taking the stand. After just six hours of deliberation, the jury reached a verdict: guilty on all counts. "This trial has revealed that Raniere, who portrayed himself as a savant and a genius, was, in fact, a master manipulator, a con man, and the crime boss of a cultlike organization," said Federal Prosecutor Richard Donoghue following the verdict.[12]

For a number of years, NXIVM attracted a coterie of rich and famous devotees. "In my opinion, NXIVM is one of the most extreme groups I have ever dealt with in the sense of how tightly wound it is around the leader, Keith Raniere," said Rick Ross, cult specialist and executive director of the nonprofit Cult Education Institute. NXIVM was defined by its charismatic leader, who was its driving force. Without its guru, NXIVM is likely to dissipate into obscurity. Keith Raniere is due to be sentenced for his various crimes in September 2019. He faces up to life in prison.[13]

---

[1] *The Times Union*, February 12, 2012—"A Quick Primer on What NXIVM Is"

[2] *The Times Union*, August 6, 2006—"Fear and Tears After NXIVM Class"

[3] *The Post-Standard*, April 13, 2018—"NXIVM Cult Leader Keith Raniere Accused of Raping 12-year-old Girl in Upstate NY"

[4] *Niagara Falls Reporter*, February 18, 2016—"The Cult of NXIVM Series Part 13: Should There Be An Investigation By Law Enforcement?"

[5] *Democrat and Chronicle*, March 11, 2018—"Rochester Woman Battles NXIVM Leader"

[6] *Niagara Falls Reporter*, January 13, 2016—"Cult of NXIVM Series, Part 8: The Relentless Pursuit of Enemies"

[7] *The Journal News*, October 24, 2017—"Inside Secretive Group Where Women are Branded"

[8] *The Times Union*, March 27, 2018—"NXIVM Leader Arrested by FBI"

[9] *International Business Times*, April 8, 2019—"Who Is Allison Mack?"

[10] CNN, June 15, 2019—"NXIVM Trial Testimony Ends with Founder Discussing Child Sex Abuse"

[11] *The Associated Press*, June 14, 2019—"Lurid Testimony Wraps Up in Case Against Self-Help Guru"

[12] *Agence France-Presse*, June 20, 2019—"Convicted: the US Sex Cult Leader Who Attracted the Rich and Famous"

Picture Credits

The publisher would like to thank the following for their kind permission to reproduce their photographs:

(Key: a–above; b–below/bottom; c–centre; f–far; l–left; r–right; t–top)